Weave a Web ~~~~ ~~ ~~~~~~ Magic

Celebrate the days and nights of power with the magic of tarot and ritual. Perfect for both solitary and group practitioners, *Tarot for All Seasons* is the only book that combines the ancient wisdom of the tarot with the solar and lunar celebrations of the pagan Wheel of the Year.

Discover how to work with seasonal energies throughout the year to improve all areas of your life—relationships, health, finances, and career.

The twelve original tarot layouts capture the spirit of the full moon Esbats, waxing and waning moons, and the eight solar Sabbats. Several three-card spreads are also included for further advice and clarification to help you hone your tarot reading skills. Sample readings offer a way to weave a story with the cards, showing how the cards relate to one another and how the same cards can describe diverse situations in various layouts.

The seventy-eight cards of the tarot form a unique system for divination, self-discovery, and magic. From the growing darkness of Samhain to the fertility and flowers of Beltane, weave a web of tarot magic as you celebrate the ever-changing world around you and within you.

About the Author

Christine Jette (Ohio) is a registered nurse and holds a Bachelor of Arts degree in psychology. She has studied all things Goddess for the past twenty years. She is an energetic healer and professional tarot consultant, specializing in health readings. Christine teaches noncredit writing part-time at the University of Cincinnati and lives with her husband and three cats. For more information about Christine Jette, please visit her website at www.findingthe-muse.com.

To Write to the Author

If you wish to contact the author or would like more information about this book, please write to the author in care of Llewellyn Worldwide and we will forward your request. Both the author and publisher appreciate hearing from you and learning of your enjoyment of this book and how it has helped you. Llewellyn Worldwide cannot guarantee that every letter written to the author can be answered, but all will be forwarded. Please write to:

Christine Jette
℅ Llewellyn Worldwide
P.O. Box 64383, Dept. 0-7387-0105-X
St. Paul, MN 55164-0383, U.S.A.

Please enclose a self-addressed stamped envelope for reply, or $1.00 to cover costs. If outside U.S.A., enclose international postal reply coupon.

Many of Llewellyn's authors have websites with additional information and resources. For more information, please visit our website at http://www.llewellyn.com.

Tarot for All Seasons

Celebrating the Days & Nights of Power

Christine Jette

2001
Llewellyn Publications
St. Paul, Minnesota 55164-0383, U.S.A.

Tarot for All Seasons: Celebrating the Days & Nights of Power © 2001 by Christine Jette. All rights reserved. No part of this book may be used or repro-
duced in any manner whatsoever, including Internet usage, without written
permission from Llewellyn Publications except in the case of brief quotations
embodied in critical articles and reviews.

FIRST EDITION
First Printing, 2001

Book design and editing by Karin Simoneau
Cover design by Lisa Novak
Interior art by Carrie Westfall

The tarot cards used on the cover of this book are from *The Robin Wood
Tarot*, © 1991 by Robin Wood.

Library of Congress Cataloging-in-Publication Data
Jette, Christine, 1953-
    Tarot for all seasons : celebrating the days & nights of power /
    Christine Jette.
        p. cm.
    Includes bibliographical references and index.
    ISBN 0-7387-0105-X
    1. Tarot. I. Title.

BF1879.T2 J48 2001
133.3'2424—dc21   2001038204

Llewellyn Worldwide does not participate in, endorse, or have any authority
or responsibility concerning private business transactions between our
authors and the public.

All mail addressed to the author is forwarded but the publisher cannot,
unless specifically instructed by the author, give out an address or phone
number.

Any Internet references contained in this work are current at publication
time, but the publisher cannot guarantee that a specific location will continue to be maintained. Please refer to the publisher's website for links to
authors' websites and other sources.

Llewellyn Publications
A Division of Llewellyn Worldwide, Ltd.
P.O. Box 64383, Dept. 0-7387-0105-X
St. Paul, MN 55164-0383, U.S.A.
www.llewellyn.com

 Printed on recycled paper in the United States of America

Also by Christine Jette

Tarot Shadow Work
Tarot for the Healing Heart

Forthcoming

Making Money with Tarot

For Mary—
I'll always treasure our trip to Salem and Samhain by the sea.

Contents

Illustrations

Preface

Magic in the Air

Mother Goddess is reawakening and we can begin to discover our primal birthright, the sheer intoxicating joy of being alive.

—STARHAWK

Before you begin . . .

The Goddess danced across the earth before time began. This ancient presence is known as Gaia, Mother Earth, Luna, Cybele, Aradia, Ishtar, Diana, Astarte, Isis, Athena, and a hundred other names. The Goddess flows in constantly moving spirals. She brings forth life and takes it back again into Her womb to be reborn. Power and strength are in Her bosom. Creativity, abundance, healing, and wisdom are Her gifts.

Playing with tarot cards is a simple but powerful way to create a seasonal connection with the Mother. We can honor the days and nights of power with tarot images and other festivities. The universal pictures of tarot awaken an inner knowing and we begin to recognize the profound meaning of the seasons. When we embrace the never-ending cycle of life, death, and rebirth, we are free to celebrate the joy of being alive in the moment of the present season.

No prior knowledge of the tarot cards is required to use this book. Chapter 1, "Merry Meet," covers the history, mystery, and lore of the Sabbats, Esbats, and tarot. Chapter 2, "As Above, So Below," explores ritual design, how to use the cards for group wisdom, how to get the most from sample readings, and how to throw three-card spreads for more information about any card in a layout. In chapter 3, "Enchanted Nights: The Esbats," you will find the new, full, and dark moon spreads.

Chapter 4, "The Cycling of Time: Darkness Into Light," offers layouts for Samhain through Ostara. Chapter 5, "Completing the Wheel: Day Into Night," completes the Wheel of the Year with layouts for Beltane through Mabon. Sample readings follow every spread in the book. "A Year and a Day," chapter 6, concludes our journey with ideas on how to dedicate yourself to the magical study of tarot. For your convenience, appendix A, "Engaging the Magic of Self-Discovery," lists the meanings of all the tarot cards.

The Goddess offers joy and affirmation of the spirit to those who go forth boldly. Join Her now as you explore the sacred days and nights of power through the magic of tarot.

1

Merry Meet

Do you believe in an invisible reality behind appearances?

— DION FORTUNE

The Wheel of the Year

The witches' calendar consists of eight important dates, called *Sabbats*. While the origins of the word "sabbat" remain obscure, it probably comes from a Hebrew word meaning "sacred, holy, or he rested."[1] Sabbats are celebrations and festivals of power.

Four of these Sabbats—Samhain, on October 31; Imbolc, on February 2; Beltane, on April 30; and Lughnasadh, or Lammas, on August 1—were originally held to celebrate the farming cycle, which was the foundation of an agricultural society.

The other four Sabbats follow the path of the sun, consisting of two solstices and two equinoxes. The two solstices denote the time of the year when the sun reaches its lowest and highest points: winter solstice, or Yule, circa December 21 or 22; and summer solstice, called Midsummer or Litha, which is around June 21.

The two equinoxes designate the time when the sun passes over the equator: the spring/vernal equinox, or Ostara, circa March 21; and the fall/autumnal equinox, or Mabon, which is around September 21 or 22. Together, these eight ritual occasions compose the cycling of time known as the Wheel of the Year.

The eight Sabbats, combined with the twelve to thirteen full moons that appear yearly, are the origins of the twenty-one Wiccan ritual occasions. Many of these pagan Sabbats survive today in both the religious and secular forms. May Day, Halloween, Groundhog Day, and Thanksgiving are all connected to ancient pagan worship.

Even the Christian holidays of Christmas and Easter derive their timing and many of their customs (such as Yule logs and coloring eggs) from pagan tradition. Easter is observed on the first Sunday after the first full moon after the spring equinox. The words "Easter," "Ostara," and "estrus" (ovulation) share the same origin: the Latin word *oestrus,* which means "frenzy." [2]

Sadly, some of the old pagan festivals have been stripped of their once sacred qualities. Samhain, a most holy Day of the Dead, has degenerated into the secular version of Halloween, depicted by hags with warts, dreadful looking ghouls, and increased candy sales; Yule, and the corresponding Christian holiday of Christmas, is a time of fierce commercialism. But the old magic remains for those who will observe it, and witches celebrate the sacred days and nights of power.

The Esbats

While the Sabbats are solar rituals, the twelve to thirteen full moon rituals each year are called *Esbats.* They occur every twenty-eight and one-fourth days. "Esbat" probably comes from the French word *s'ebattre,* meaning "to frolic or have a good time." [3]

Every two to three years there is an extra moon, or thirteenth lunar month, appearing as two full moons during one month. This thirteenth Esbat, called "Blue Moon," is the second full moon of the month and is considered most powerful—a time for magical workings of all types, especially protection, purification, and healing.

During the Esbats, witches gather to honor the Goddess. The moon symbolizes the Goddess, or "She Who Is," and is a source of powerful energy. Because of this larger amount of energy during the full moon, witches practice magic and cast spells "for the good of all, harm none." Think of an Esbat as the witch's "working holiday."

During the Esbats, witches slow down, exchange news, reconnect with the Goddess, take care of business, and observe important rites of passage such as handfastings (weddings). Inner teachings of the Old Religion are studied and there is usually dancing, singing, and lots of good food.

History and Mystery of the Tarot

The origins of the tarot cards have long been lost in the distant past. The oldest, most complete pack on record is the Italian Visconti deck, dating back to about 1450 C.E. Opinions about the tarot's origins vary greatly and are often a subject of hot dispute among tarot scholars. Go to a library or bookstore and start reading about the history of the tarot cards. You will be amazed at the differences of opinion. I find the tarot's obscure beginnings to be delightful because it adds to the veiled mystery of the cards I love.

Whether you believe the tarot's origin is from Gypsy fortunetellers, or a playful pastime of the Renaissance rich and famous, one thing is clear: Tarot cards, once fully studied and understood, can reveal important messages and insights to help us go forward with our lives.

It's All In the Cards

A complete tarot deck has seventy-eight cards. Twenty-two cards, numbered 0–21, make up the Major Arcana, the Fool through the World. The other fifty-six cards, known as the Minor Arcana, are divided into four suits of fourteen cards each, numbered 1–10, plus the Court Cards—Pages, Knights, Queens, and Kings. Ones are called Aces, just like a modern deck of playing cards. Sometimes the

Minor Arcana cards are illustrated, as are all the Major Arcana cards, and sometimes they have only the symbol of their suits.

The four suits symbolize the four natural elements, the four planes of existence, the four directions, and the four seasons.

Suit of Wands: Fire/ Creative Inspiration/ South/ Spring

Suit of Cups: Water/ Emotions/ West/ Summer

Suit of Swords: Air/ Intellect/ East/ Autumn

Suit of Pentacles: Earth/ Materialism/ North/ Winter

Note: In some books, this order differs—the suit of Cups is placed first, representing spring. I choose to list it this way because all life begins with an initial creative spark. No spark, no life.

Because over one hundred decks are available today, many variations exist. Some decks, such as *Daughters of the Moon,* exclude male imagery. Other decks have different names for their suits. For instance, Wands may be called Crystals, or Pentacles may be referred to as Discs or Coins. Court Cards, the "people of tarot," can be named differently, too—Kings appearing as Shamans is one example.

You will also find astrological associations assigned to the Major Arcana or Court Cards. The most common combination is tarot and the mystical Kabbala, or Tree of Life. One of my personal favorites is the correlation of Jungian archetypes with the tarot. If you are committed to learning the tarot, then read, study, ask questions, and *decide for yourself* about types of decks and relationships of the cards to other esoteric study.

Numbering is important in tarot, and the numbers one through ten carry the same meanings throughout, but are expressed differently through their suits. For example, the Ace (or One) means new beginnings, but the Ace of Cups is emotional beginnings, and the Ace of Wands is creative or inspirational beginnings. Incidentally, cards numbered one through ten are sometimes called "pip" cards.

In the Major Arcana, if numbers larger than ten are reduced, the result is, amazingly, the essence of the card; for instance, card 17, The Star, can be reduced to eight (1 + 7 = 8). Eights imply regeneration or new ways forward, and that is certainly true of the Star. Here is a brief summary of the numerical associations of the cards, but remember, opinions vary on this, too:

1: Beginnings, potential

2: Balance or the need to balance

3: Expansion, growth

4: Stability or stagnation

5: Conflict, struggle, challenge

6: Harmony, cooperation

7: Inner work, awakening

8: Regeneration, new ways forward

9: Completion (or foundation)

10: Starting over at a higher cycle

Note: In some books, Nine is integration of experience and Ten is completion.

Appendix A offers just one woman's opinion on the meaning of all seventy-eight cards. Refer to it if you are new to tarot, but for goodness sake, don't take my definitions as the last word. We all come from a different frame of reference about life. I don't know how many tarot books I have read in my lifetime, but I do know I have learned something valuable in every one. Pick and choose. Decide what makes sense to you and discard the rest. Use the "definitions" in appendix A as a launching point for contemplation, but study *many* tarot books over time, and trust your intuition.

The Major Arcana
(Greater Secrets)

The Major Arcana, numbers 0–21, the Fool through the World, speak to you of both life lessons and life wisdom: those qualities being tested and developed, your gifts and challenges, karma, and the reasons you are here. The twenty-two cards symbolize spiritual development and help you understand your place in the world. The "greater secrets" will point to the higher overview of life and give you insights into the "big picture." They will also hint at your healing potential.

The Minor Arcana
(Lesser Secrets)

The Minor Arcana, or "lesser secrets," offer information along the planes of existence: Wands, spiritual creativity in everyday life; Cups, emotions and feelings; Swords, psychological well-being/the mind; and Pentacles, physical reality and the body.

When the different suits shows up in a reading, ask yourself, *What action can I take?* (Wands); *What am I feeling or dreaming about?* (Cups); *What am I thinking or what decision needs to be made?* (Swords). Because Pentacles explore issues of food, housing, money, work, the body, and physical health, ask yourself, *What do I value?*

In life, there is no separation between body, emotion, mind, and spirit. It is impossible for something to happen to us without all four levels of existence being affected. Likewise, it is impossible to change without attending to these four levels of being. Life does not fall neatly into categories. Because stress or concerns at any level affect all levels, the lines sometimes blur. Appendix A serves as a general guide as you begin the wonderful process of self-discovery.

Court Cards
(The People and Personalities of Tarot)

No other cards in the tarot deck have more interpretations. Read any tarot book and you'll find different meanings and names. These sixteen cards can be challenging because you have to decide if they represent another person, an aspect of yourself, or both. I'll make it simple: The Court Cards are *always a reflection of you*—you draw the people to you that *you* need for *your* life wisdom. So, it doesn't matter if it describes someone else—the card is still about *you* and *your* need to have those qualities in your life.

We all have qualities that are traditionally associated with masculine and feminine ways of being. For instance, a woman can be competitive and a man can be nurturing. Be aware that the King and Knight can represent a woman and the Queen can symbolize a man. The gender, or "occupation," of the card is less important than the *qualities* it describes.

Pages can represent a child, but they also introduce the element of their suit, the willingness to change, risk, or learn something new. Pages can symbolize the catalyst needed for change and the child within us all. Pages also carry messages related to their suit: telephone calls or significant e-mail (Page of Wands); important dreams (Page of Cups); written warnings (Page of Swords); and messages from your body, especially in the form of illness—what is your body trying to tell you? (Page of Pentacles).

Knights represent young adults or someone starting over, focusing on a specific task through their suit, be it creative (Wands), emotional (Cups), psychological (Swords), or physical (Pentacles). Our "knightly" qualities include being energetic, daring, headstrong, and goal oriented. Knights show movement and action through their suit.

Queens are mature. They take their understanding of life inward and use this life wisdom to nurture others and encourage self-development through their specific suit; for example, the Queen of Cups nurtures the emotions. Because they are the embodiment of the feminine tradition of healing, Queens often represent healing in relationship to their suit. An example of this is the Queen of Pentacles symbolizing a natural healer. Our "queenly" qualities include sensitivity, fullness of expression, empathy, and personal, inner control.

Kings are also mature, but they project their maturity outward in the form of leadership through their suit. They take charge and give advice: creative or spiritual advice (King of Wands); emotional advice (King of Cups); psychological or intellectual advice (King of Swords); and practical advice about the everyday world (King of Pentacles, especially in the area of finances or work). Our "kingly" qualities include being capable and in control, with an air of authority, leadership, and worldliness.

Reversed Cards and the 8–11 Difference

Some decks show Strength as card 8, and Justice as card 11; other decks reverse it—Justice is 8 and Strength is 11. *Tarot for All Seasons* is an application of tarot—one more way to use the cards for personal enrichment. Because it is not a basic tarot "textbook," it does not deal with the 8–11 and reversed card controversies.

Among tarot authors, reversed card meanings in a layout cause an even greater controversy than the tarot's origins. Much has been written about both subjects. Mary K. Greer explains it beautifully in *Tarot for Your Self*, and *Choice Centered Tarot*, by Gail Fairfield, clarifies the dilemma with eloquent simplicity.

For the purposes of celebrating days and nights of power, it does not matter whether your deck has Strength or Justice as number 8. The nuance of the card remains the same. If a card appears reversed (upside down) in one of the spreads, interpret it as a sign of its importance. In effect, a reversed card says to you, "Hey, look at me first! I'm important because I am different." It draws attention to itself and may signify "the need for" that quality in its position.

A reversed card can also be operating on a deeply psychological or unconscious level, with its significance not yet apparent to you. Be patient. Its meaning will become clear as you work with the cards. This is sufficient information about reversed cards and will be enough to get you started with seasonal tarot work. Because many tarot readers find the reversed card interpretations helpful, I have included them in appendix A for your convenience. Experiment. Read. Decide for yourself what makes sense to you.

Doom and Gloom for Thirty Dollars

It is important to emphasize that there is no such thing as "good" or "bad" tarot cards. They symbolize a spectrum of life experiences and *every* card presents an opportunity to learn and grow. The Wheel of the Year turns and we change with it. The cyclical pattern of birth, growth, maturation, decay, death, and rebirth is the dance of life, with all its attending joys and sorrows.

When we have a run of bad luck in our lives, we are vulnerable to the suggestion of curses or hexes. *Why is this happening?* We want it to stop. *Anyone* who tries to turn your fears against you (to make you more afraid) is out to control you, not help you.

The moment a reader predicts doom and gloom, hexes, or a "preordained" disaster that leaves you feeling powerless, get out of there as fast as possible and do not pay! No one, and I mean *no one*, has that kind of power over your life without you handing it over to him first.

Nothing in tarot is preordained. We always have the power to change trends through responsible choice. For example, say a reader tells you that you will die of a heart attack. If you have unhealthful habits, you can either do nothing to change your lifestyle and kick off as predicted, or you can give up those cigarettes, stop eating fifty grams of fat a day, and see a healthcare professional for a checkup. It's your choice.

It is the responsibility of the reader to be honest. If she truly sees a catastrophic event, such as loss of income or serious illness, she certainly needs to be candid, but her role is to assist you, not scare you to death. When catastrophe does strike, you will be better prepared because you have examined possible reactions to it ahead of time. A worthwhile tarot reading empowers you to face change with courage.

Tarot Is a Reflection of You

Tarot is a mirror extension of yourself because your life is a reflection of your beliefs. Interpretation is in the eye of the beholder. Because of this, *Tarot for All Seasons* does not ascribe to one type of deck. Work with any deck that appeals to you.

Every tarot card conveys information through its activity, color, scene, people, or attitude. Tarot symbols affect our perceptions and activate our inner selves. The art of tarot shows forces and circumstances that have been active in our lives at one time or another.

Approach tarot as the picture book of your life story. The "art" of a tarot reading lies within the symbols of the cards. You "read" a card by comparing the images to events in your own life. Does a card remind you of a situation, event, relationship, or method of communicating? You can learn many things about yourself by attending to the symbolism of tarot on a regular basis. Approach tarot with heart, and your mind will follow.

The key to understanding tarot is to allow it to come to life. The sooner you connect a card with a real situation, the sooner you become a skilled interpreter. For example, if you are feeling depressed and the Four of Cups appears in a reading, look at the picture on the card and *feel* the depression. When you see it again in another layout, you will remember the feeling and know its meaning without memorizing anything.

Always look at the card with which you are working. No amount of memorization can replace the artistic symbolism of the picture. Connecting to a picture is the fastest way to learn tarot, no matter which deck you are using.

It is important to get a basic idea of traditional meanings because this will keep you out of fantasy and wishful thinking. It is also important to give your intuitive self some latitude because this keeps you out of rigidity. You probably trust your intellect, but learning to respect and trust your *intuition* is the focus of celebrating the seasons with tarot.

Now to the burning question: Can you really read for yourself? Of course. Reading for yourself can be a rich source of insight. Be aware of the potential for wishful thinking. Because your own concerns may interfere, the fortunetelling aspect of tarot may be less reliable. If you are too emotionally involved with an issue, do a reading for yourself and then have a reading done for you to compare. Talk it over with a trusted friend or adviser to get a "reality check."

Meditation and Tarot

Meditation allows you to quiet your mind and access your inner wisdom. It can also strengthen your spiritual connection. The greatest aid to meditation is your intention to still the mind. The easiest way to do this is to concentrate on slow, deep breathing until you feel your entire body relax. If your mind wanders, simply bring it back to your slow, deep breathing.

If you are skilled at seeing pictures in your mind's eye, imagine a beautiful nature scene. It can be a forest, a beach, or any place you prefer, as long as you find it restful. Imagery such as this can take you to a peaceful place where you are calm, and the mind gradually becomes still. Chanting and sounds made on instruments such as drums or bells can be powerful focal points for meditation, and so can your tarot cards.

Try this: Select any tarot card you like. Prop it in front of you so you can see it without straining your eyes. Take slow, deep breaths until you feel yourself relax. Breathe out worries and pain; breathe in a feeling of well-being. When you are relaxed, look at your chosen tarot card. Concentrate on breathing in a slow, deep rhythm. Attend to whatever thoughts come into your mind as you gaze at the picture.

Mentally converse with the card. Ask it about its meaning in your life. Strong feelings toward a card—both positive and negative—usually signal that the card holds an important message for you. Let your thoughts flow. If your critical censor shouts at you about the silliness of talking to a tarot card, tell it to be quiet and bring your attention back to deep breathing. Stay with the card for awhile and your inner wisdom will whisper to you.

Your Tarot Journal

Keeping a journal allows you to put into words your innermost thoughts without fear of criticism. A journal is your personal property and can be kept confidential, much like a diary. Many beautiful blank books are available, but you need not spend a lot of money on your journal. A three-ring notebook is adequate, and you can add entries on loose-leaf paper. Perhaps you'll want to decorate the outside of your notebook. Creativity unlocks intuition—make the journal a unique expression of you.

The benefit of keeping a tarot journal comes from the process of writing your thoughts, feelings, insights, and observances. You can be sad, silly, angry, profane, or anything else you want to be without fear of reprisal. The journal becomes the chronicle of your life story. Whether you share it with anyone is up to you. As you reread entries, you will find the journal to be a record of growth, wisdom, healing—and magic.

If you notice some of the cards repeating themselves in your seasonal layouts, there is a message calling for your attention. A theme in your life, represented by the repetitive cards, needs examination. Sometimes the cards' messages are not immediately clear. By keeping a tarot journal, you can review confusing readings next week, next month, or next Sabbat. You may be surprised at how much sense the cards make at a later date.

Honor all information you receive, regardless of whether you grasp it today. Adopt an attitude of respectful regard and do not dismiss cards you don't like or don't understand. The message is in the cards—*if you stay with the cards.* Over time, with patience and practice, the puzzle pieces will fall into place.

Journal entries can be jotted down at odd moments, but you may want to establish a regular time for writing about your tarot experiences through the seasons. Once the value of journal keeping has been established, you will find it becomes a trusted friend—a valuable ritual during which you record your feelings, traumas, pain, joy, triumphs, and insights.

Record and date every seasonal tarot layout and keep it in your journal. With each reading, you are one step further in your journey toward wisdom. Keeping a record over time allows you to monitor your inner development and observe the miracle of the Wheel of the Year—and your ability to change with it.

Ritual and Tarot: Deciding What You Value

It is confusing to pick up six different tarot books and read six different ways to handle and store the cards. You can drive yourself crazy trying to do everything you read in a book. The purpose of a ritual is to help you focus on the task at hand, and opinions vary on what to do with tarot decks. So how do you decide whether or not to clear the cards with moonlight, face north while working with them, shuffle only to the right, burn clary sage, wrap them in silk, or store the cards in a pine box filled with crystals?

Rituals are personal. If you like rituals and they help you concentrate on working with the cards, use them. No ritual you do is sacred unless it is sacred to you. If you develop a habit because it centers your attention or signals your intuition, then it has value. *The most powerful rituals are the ones invented by you.* Never do something because a book tells you to do it, including this book! Listen to and trust your inner wisdom. Be aware of why you do what you do. Use whatever ritual feels right when working with the cards.

In *Tarot for All Seasons,* you will not be told how to shuffle, deal, clean, or store your deck. It's your choice. Read about ritual and tarot in several books and then decide for yourself. Treat the cards the way you treat anything else of value. Tarot can be a powerful tool for accessing inner wisdom, but the magic does not come from the cards—the magic comes from *you.*

2

As Above, So Below

*Every dance I danced, every childlike chase, every handful of flowers,
was a bonding of my heart and my spirit with my Mother, the Earth.*

—LAURIE CABOT

Earth, Air, Fire, and Water

Whether lunar ritual (Esbat), or solar celebration (Sabbat), chapters 3, 4, and 5 follow the simple format of this chapter. Use the basic ritual design given and build upon it with the specific correspondences found with each lunar or solar layout. For each moon phase and season, you will need the following items: a deck of tarot cards, incense, herbs or oil attuned to the moon phase or season, herbal tea or fruit juice, a candle, and the time required to awaken to the experience. Remember that no ritual you perform is sacred unless it is sacred to you.

Use fresh flowers and herbs, crytals and stones, incense, or oil to charge the atmosphere with your magical intentions of the season. Each ritual offers suggestions, but trust your intuition. Place your chosen items on an altar or in your sacred space. Go where your heart leads as you embrace the days and nights of power through the magic of tarot.

The Ritual

Witches take a purifying bath, ground, center, cast the circle of protection, call the quarters, recite a blessing chant, and invoke the Goddess or God as preliminary (and protective) steps to ritual work. Proper ritual closure is also necessary to release unwanted or excess energy. The solar and lunar energies are powerful and real. Acquaint yourself with these important protective steps before undertaking ritual work during the Esbats and Sabbats. Scott Cunningham's book *Wicca: A Guide for the Solitary Practitioner* or Silver RavenWolf's book *To Ride a Silver Broomstick* are good places to start.

The ritual creates a place in time where you can honor and communicate with the mystery of the Goddess in Her season. In this place between the worlds, desire and destiny and the spiritual and material become one. Sit comfortably in a quiet place, free of distractions. Breathe deeply. As you concentrate on your deep breaths, allow yourself to feel at ease and in the present moment.

Into the candle's glow, focus your intention to realize your desire and visualize it as reality. Verbally affirm its truth as you gaze at the flame. State out loud that your desire be for the good of all, according to free will, harming no one. For an extra boost, add "it's equivalent or better," because you never know what the Goddess has planned for you.

When you feel your ritual is complete, release its outcome from your grasp. Relax and allow the universe to manifest your desires. Your pure intention will generate its own power. To close the ritual, give thanks to the Goddess and extinguish the candle. If you choose to let the candle burn down, attend to fire safety.

The Tarot Cards

The cards represent your intention. They are your earthly connection to your spirit's desire. As you hold a card in your hand, invest your intention to realize your dreams. Carry it with you to maintain a connection to the mystery of the Goddess, where dreams, desire, and destiny become one according to Her season.

You can leave the cards or layout on your altar for awhile. Inner wisdom develops over time. Record new insights in a journal. Date each entry and reread them the following week, month, or Sabbat. You will be amazed at their accuracy.

The Scent

The scent represents the ethereal presence of the Goddess. Allow the fragrance to enter and leave your consciousness. Breathe in and become present in the season's moment. Breathe out and release doubt and fear.

The Magical Brew

Wine has long been used in magical and religious rites. For those who wish to avoid the use of alcohol, the Goddess offers you hidden gifts. An herbal tea attunes you to Her seasons. Savor its aroma, flavor, and power while you hold magic and mystery in a cup.

A word to the wise: Although adverse reactions to the common herbs suggested in this book are rare, it is best to treat any herbal substance with caution and respect.

The Candle

The candle symbolizes you. Its color is the seasonal focal point of your pure intention to manifest your desires. The flame of the candle represents your spirit. Its warmth is a reminder of your true nature. Its brightness is a reflection of you and your clarity of intention. The flame, as your spirit, remains constant throughout the Wheel of the Year.

Awakening to the Experience

Words have power, and what we send out comes back to us (at least) threefold. As Shakti Gawain writes, "An affirmation is a strong positive statement that something is already so. It is a way of making firm that which you are imagining."[1]

You draw to you those people and events that mirror your own state of consciousness. Like attracts like. What is going on around you reflects your personal energies. Awaken to the experience of the season and proclaim your positive desires. The universe will enthusiastically support you.

Your own words work best, but until you find your voice, you can borrow mine: "I am fully present in the place of mystery where desire and destiny become one. Into this clearing of pure energy, I awaken to the experience of *(season)*. I embrace life, without fear or limitation. This, or something better, is manifesting for me now, for the good of all, harming no one, according to free will. And so it is." (Witches usually end with "So mote it be," but I simply don't like the word "mote." If you are comfortable with this phrase, by all means use it.)

Group Wisdom

Tarot for All Seasons can be used in solitary or group celebrations. If you use the layouts for group wisdom, the cards illuminate group characteristics. They will describe the group and then offer insights into group dynamics, advising you on what to release, what to keep and nurture, and the direction to take. Rituals vary greatly and are meant to be personal. Use the suggestions presented here to spark your own playful imagination.

Getting the Most from Sample Readings

Tarot readings weave together a narrative story of your life based on the question you ask, the position of the cards, and the relationships of the cards to each other. A reading will usually describe a situation or give you advice about a situation.

We all read the cards differently based on our personal life experiences. To get the most from the sample readings, compare your style and interpretation of the cards to what is presented after each case history. Read the case history and look at the spread before reading my interpretation.

First, decide for yourself the meaning of each spread. Try to imagine that the seeker is coming to you for a reading. Make your own notes about the sample spread, then compare your interpretation to mine. Write down the alternative courses of action that each spread suggests to you.

The beauty of tarot is that it is a reflection of each of us. If we stay true to our own intuitive, spiritual voice, both readings (yours and mine) will be accurate, even if they are different.

I'd like to thank the seekers who allowed me to base the sample readings in truth. Ninety-nine percent of my clients are women. Because the sample readings are based in fact, all the case histories involve female querents. Their names have been changed to protect confidentiality. (A "seeker" or "querent" is the person having the tarot reading done. I prefer the term "client," but that's a personal choice.)

Depth Readings

A three-card reading is an effective way to get more information from any layout in this book. You can do a three-card spread for summarizing the entire layout, for one position in the layout that is especially puzzling, or if you need a time frame. When you are "stuck" on the meaning of a particular spread or a specific card in a seasonal spread, shuffle the remaining deck and lay your cards out as shown in figure 1.

This three-card reading is helpful when a card is difficult to interpret:

Card 1: Illusion. Hidden material. It may be fantasy, wishful thinking, or unconscious hopes and fears. This card reveals truth that is just beginning to surface and will soon become known to you. You may now be vaguely aware of these forces at work.

Card 2: Knowledge. This card reveals what you really want and what you are aware of wanting.

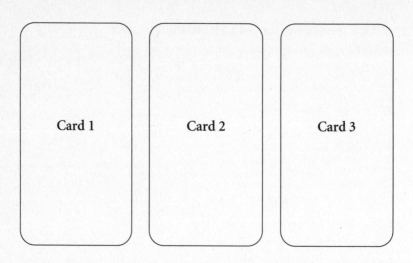

Figure 1: Three-Card Reading for Depth

Card 3: Magic. Focused will remains the core of magic. This card shows a conceivable outcome—the future that you can create by the deliberate act of stating your intention and focusing your will on your stated desires. It does not show what is, but what *can be* when you focus. Card three gives you the power to change trends in a reading.

Try another three-card layout that works well for summarizing a reading. (Lay your cards out as shown in figure 1.)

Card 1: Blocks. What is difficult in the present situation.

Card 2: Strengths. What is helpful in the present situation.

Card 3: Advice. The next step. What to do about a situation.

Finally, use this three-card spread when you need a time frame on your reading (again, lay your cards out as shown in figure 1).

Card 1: The Present. The situation as it is right now.

Card 2: The Near Future. Shows trends for the next one to three months.

Card 3: Far Future: Shows trends for the next four to twelve months.

In my experience as a professional reader, I have found that it is useless to "predict" farther than a period of one year. Too many things can happen to alter circumstances. Tarot cards give us an opportunity to look at a situation in a different light, but they do not predict a fixed or fated future.

The future can be affected by the past, and the choices we make today can certainly have an influence on the future, but the future is not preordained. The cards suggest tendencies and influences given the current circumstances, but we always have the power of choice in the present moment; we can take action today that will change and improve the course of future events.

Please remember the Threefold Law when making plans, casting spells, working with any of these Goddesses, or attuning to the seasons: Energy is neutral; its power lies in the *intent* of the sender. Whatever you send out, for good or ill, will come back to you (at least) three times stronger. If you seek to do harm, you will be harmed. Vengeful, selfish, or malicious intent destroys the sender, not the recipient. Be certain your intent is pure, for the good of all, harming no one, according to free will.

This is the moment for the Goddess's return, carrying with Her the torch of truth, light, and love. Journey now into the realms of wonder, magic, and divinity.

3

Enchanted Nights: The Esbats

The Moon is the Goddess of the Night, Mistress of our dreams and emotions, and witness to our deepest secrets.

—SUSAN BOWES

The Full Moon

The Mother Goddess provides for and nourishes the earth, and Her time is during the full moon Esbat. She is called Demeter, Isis, Ceres, Freya, Ishtar, Cerridwen, Inanna, and other names. The Great Mother represents the body as vessel, childbearing, and nurturance. She is fertile, creative, menstruating, and living in her prime.

Call upon Her during your Esbat ritual for manifesting your goals, for blessings, for protection (no one protects like a mother protecting her young), for growing, for making choices, for ease of childbirth, for protection of animals, for creativity, and for spiritual direction.

The Full Moon (Esbat) Ritual

The Esbat is a time for powerful magical workings because the Great Mother is in Her brimming intensity. Her season is summer, and the full moon is Her monthly point of power. Witches also honor Her on Beltane, Midsummer, and Lughnasadh. On Yule, the Goddess in all Her phases is honored as Maiden, Mother, and Crone.

Full moon rituals can involve anything from asking for blessings and protection to seeking spiritual direction and developing psychic gifts. Cauldrons, wooden spoons, holey stones, baskets, malachite, red jasper, and objects or coins made of silver and rose or clear quartz add power to your full moon ritual. Please refer to chapter 2 for basic ritual design.

The Full Moon (Great Mother) Tarot Cards

The Empress (card 3) symbolizes the Great Mother and signifies a time to manifest your desires in relationship to others. Creativity, motherhood, nurturance, love, abundance, art, family, and sensuality belong to Her.

All Queens offer fullness of expression through their suits: Queen of Wands, creativity and action; Queen of Cups, depth of emotion and psychic gifts; Queen of Swords, introspection, strength, communication, and intellectual pursuits; Queen of Pentacles, sensuality, loyalty, patience, fertility, and trust.

The Moon (card 18) gives you an opportunity to experience the mystery of the Goddess. Place the Moon on the altar if you wish for "lunar consciousness" (developing deep trust in your feelings, knowing that solutions may be intuitive rather than logical).

The Scents of the Mother

Rose, gardenia, ambergris, jasmine, peach, or pear. Cinnamon reflects the potency of Her creative powers. Sandalwood is all-purpose for any phase of the moon.

Magical Brews of the Mother

Apricot or pear nectar, lemonade, jasmine, rosebud, cinnamon, or peach tea.

Candles of the Mother

Red for creativity and passion, rose for love, silver to reflect Her mystery, white for protection and purity of intention.

Moontime

Magic is afoot. Because the full moon is a time for powerful, magical workings of all types, the Moontime spread covers a wide range of possibilities. D. J. Conway writes in her book *Maiden, Mother, Crone,* "As the Mother of All, She is our will to live, to accomplish, to reproduce, and to establish peace. She lives in all Her creations and creatures, as we do in Her." [1]

Use the Moontime spread to give you an overview of your heart's desires. If you have a specific question in mind, ask your question as you shuffle the cards. For more information about the Moontime layout, or a specific card in the layout, use one of the three-card spreads found in chapter 2.

Breathe deeply and shuffle your deck. Lay the cards out in positions one through seven, as shown in figure 2. The cards reflect the increasing moon into the fullness of the Mother.

Position 1: Relationships. What you need to know now about developing your potential in relationship to others. The truth of your current relationships, be they lover, coworker, family, or friend.

Position 2: The Power of Choice. What decision needs to be made now to fully express your potential? What will free your creativity?

Position 3: Manifesting Goals. What action do you need to take on the physical plane to reinforce your magical workings? What can you do in the mundane world to support your spirit's desire?

Position 4: Creativity. The Mother has given you talents, abilities, and gifts. What must you do to fully express them? If you don't like this card, it is because the card shows blocks that you need to address before you can realize your full creative gifts.

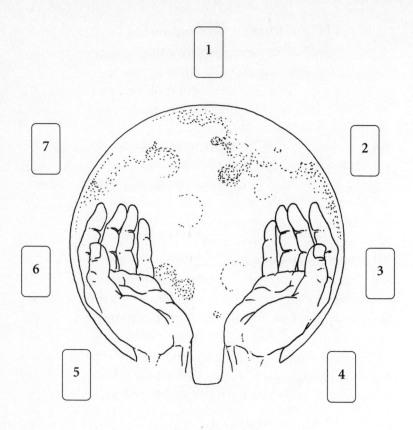

Figure 2: Moontime

Position 5: Protection. Shows you where to establish personal boundaries so you do not give your power away. What do you need to protect?

Position 6: Psychic Gifts. How can you best develop your intuition? If position six is a Court Card, it suggests the appearance of a teacher, guide, or mentor.

Position 7: Blessings and Spiritual Direction. The Mother wants you to celebrate the joy of being alive. What do you have to be thankful for? How can you best express the Goddess in you?

To complete the Moontime reading, you can meditate with the cards, write a journal entry, keep the cards on the altar until the next full moon, or simply close. Carry a card or two with you during the day to strengthen the connection between you and the fruition of your spirit's desire. Affirm your personal power to express the Goddess in you: "I awaken to the Goddess in Her prime and am fully capable of creating the life I want. This, or something better, is manifesting for me now, for the good of all, harming no one, according to free will. So must it be."

Sample Moontime Reading

Jean is an attractive young woman whose life is troubled. She works in a custom-frame shop and is a skilled painter. Her dream of having her own gallery one day seems like an impossibility because she has a small boy from a failed marriage and few financial resources. She lives with a controlling partner named David for one reason—he has money and the apartment they share is lovely, in a good part of town. She knows she could never afford anything comparable on her own small income.

Jean is not happy with her situation, but until she can figure out her next move, she stays in the relationship because her partner buys things for her son that she cannot. Jean has decided to overlook David's behavior in favor of financial security—for now. Still, she knows things could be better, so she does a Moontime spread for powerful advice.

Position 1: Seven of Swords. Jean knows the Seven describes her relationship with David. She would like to get closer to him, but the truth is, she doesn't trust him. She senses he is hiding his true feelings and she knows she hasn't been open with her own. Every time she tries to initiate a meaningful conversation, it either ends in anger or dissolves into small talk. The Seven reminds her that nothing is accomplished by aggression. If she wants clear communication with David, she must remember to be levelheaded, or at least tactful, and keep her emotions in check.

Position 2: The Devil. When Jean sees this card, she immediately knows she has been too attached to material security, especially with the lavish gifts that David buys her son. The truth is, she's unhappy in the relationship, but is afraid to leave because she's never been alone. At the moment, she must choose between material comfort and spiritual growth.

All her energy is spent either quarreling with David or fretting about the relationship. She has no energy left to think creatively. The Devil asks Jean to look at her material attachments and face her fears of being alone. When she can do these two things, she is promised tremendous growth and a release of creative energy.

Position 3: Eight of Wands. Jean has been casting spells for financial freedom, but has not done anything on the material plane to support her magical workings. The Eight of Wands asks Jean to broaden her horizons. This card marks the end of delays and a period of stagnation, but only if she takes action on her own behalf. The Eight of Wands urges Jean to try out new ideas and begin new projects.

If she wants to move closer to her dream of owning an art gallery, the Eight tells her that now is the time to take steps toward it. She can begin by looking for work at an art museum or established gallery. The Eight of Wands suggests that she will quickly gain the experience she needs to move her one step closer to her goal and, by acting quickly, she will successfully promote herself. The card also warns Jean that the time to act on inspirations is now—the creative energy of the Eight of Wands is temporary.

Position 4: Seven of Cups. The Seven of Cups does not surprise Jean. She knows she has many talents and choices but she can't make a decision about work or her relationship with David. Jean isn't sure what the Seven of Cups is trying to specifically tell her, so she sets it aside for now. She decides to do a three-card spread for more information at the end of the reading.

Position 5: Four of Pentacles. Jean doesn't like the looks of this card at all. The Four of Pentacles tells Jean that she is clinging to everything familiar: a job, a relationship, and material possessions. Her fixed ideas of security and safety are preventing personal fulfillment, but right now she is too scared to change. The presence of fear is confirmed by the Devil in position two.

Jean also knows she is holding on to a relationship that no longer works. By doing so, she is giving her power away. Jean is seeking stability and what she has is stagnation. She realizes that she has been clinging to David because of a deep-rooted fear of abandonment. She is distressed by the painful insight but feels lighter somehow. It's as though she is seeing herself clearly for the first time. She realizes that awareness is the first step in healing. Jean decides to seek the aid of a therapist, at least for awhile, to determine the causes of her fear.

Position 6: Queen of Cups. Jean hasn't trusted her intuition for a long time. She understands now that her intuitive ability isn't dead, she just hasn't been using it. The Queen of Cups confirms Jean's decision to see a therapist, because this Queen, more than any other, is the feminine embodiment of emotional healing. The Queen of Cups reminds Jean that the key to emotional healing is learning to listen to—and trust—the intuitive voice that always knows what is best for her.

Position 7: Page of Wands. In all of her indecision, Jean has forgotten to be grateful for her son. The Page of Wands tells Jean to give thanks to the Goddess for Her beautiful creation. How lucky she feels to be blessed with her sweet boy. Jean makes a promise to the Goddess that she will pause each day to appreciate her child.

The Page of Wands is fun-loving and spiritual. He gently reminds Jean that she is taking herself too seriously. She needs to lighten up and have some fun, especially with her son. This Page promises Jean a season of spiritual rebirth if she only wakes up to it.

Sample Three-Card Reading

Jean feels empowered after the reading, but the Seven of Cups still puzzles her. She has concluded that the Seven of Cups is trying to describe an emotional block that is keeping her from the full expression of her creative energy, but what is the block? Jean decides to use a three-card spread because the Seven of Cups is difficult to interpret. As she shuffles, she asks the cards to give her the information that she needs, in the most understandable form possible, as it relates to the Seven of Cups.

Card 1: Eight of Cups. Jean has been clinging to a worn-out relationship and the financial security it offers her. Her illusion is that the relationship is working. In order to break through the fantasy, the Eight of Cups tells Jean that she needs to turn her back on the relationship and walk away, even if it makes her sad to do so. She has invested a lot of emotional energy into a situation that drains, rather than renews, her spirit. Eight is the number of regeneration and new ways forward. If Jean can let go of her illusion, she will experience an upsurge of healing, creative energy.

Card 2: Nine of Pentacles. Jean knows that she wants to be financially secure and independent. She also realizes that she feels unfulfilled at the moment. The Nine of Pentacles tells Jean that self-reliance is the key to prosperity. It promises Jean that she will be able to make her own way in the world by using her talents and abilities.

Card 3: The Lovers. At first glance, Jean thinks of David when she sees this card and is confused by it. She decides to look through a few of her tarot books for a wider interpretation of the Lovers. Jean realizes that the Lovers card is about responsible choices: decisions concerning a love affair, and a choice between security or taking a personal risk.

She knows that now is the time to make a decision about her relationship with David. The Lovers card promises that something that looks negative on the surface turns out to be a blessing in disguise. Jean knows, deep in her heart, that going it alone is the loving thing to do for all concerned.

The Lovers card suggests that her creative expression will be freed when she terminates an emotionally draining relationship. It tells Jean to decide and then move on, confident in the knowledge that her choice is the right one.

She leaves the Moontime layout on the altar to strengthen her resolve to make life-affirming choices. Jean carries the Empress with her throughout the day as a reminder that she has the power to create the life she wants.

The Maiden

The Esbats are full moon celebrations, but magical workings are appropriate during the other phases of the moon, as well. The waxing, or increasing, moon symbolizes the Maiden Goddess. She has many names—Artemis, Diana, Macha, to name but three. Regardless of Her name, the Maiden is associated with youth, first menstruation, puberty, adventures, the wilderness, and animals. She is the Lady of the Hunt.

Call upon Her for any new plans or beginnings, especially in relationships or work. She gives you a freer, more independent attitude at any stage of your life.

The Maiden Ritual

The waxing moon is a time for new beginnings of any type, especially in relationships and work. All phases of planning a new project belong to the Maiden. Call upon Her when you need the motivation to get started. The power of the Maiden is found in the pagan holidays of Imbolc and the spring equinox, or Ostara. Maiden, Mother, and Crone are honored together at Yule.

Maiden rituals can involve anything from starting school to welcoming a new child or animal into the home. The powerful creative force of the Maiden will give you a freer, more independent attitude in all aspects of your life. Any of the following items will add power to your rituals: arrows, feathers, moonstones, seeds, bulbs, a new plant, crescent moons, and objects made of pewter. Appropriate animal figurines include cats and deer.

The Maiden Tarot Cards

In tarot, all Aces offer the gift of new beginnings through their element: Ace of Wands for creativity; Ace of Cups for an upsurge of emotional or psychic energy; Ace of Swords for intellectual or mental endeavors and any type of communication; Ace of Pentacles for work, money, improving health, and manifesting on the physical plane.

The Pages, likewise, offer openness to exploration through their suit. No new beginning is complete without the Fool, which conveys a joyous trust that the universe will provide and a willingness to take the leap of faith into a new adventure. Call upon the Fool for spontaneity of action.

The Scents of the Maiden

Spring flowers, such as daisies, tulips, or daffodils; sandalwood, pine, cedar, or any deep, woodsy scent. She adores all perfume.

Magical Brews of the Maiden

Catnip, peppermint, or mugwort tea; spring water and milk. (*Caution:* While mugwort usually regulates bleeding, it may cause an increased flow in some women, especially during the menopausal change.)

Candles of the Maiden

All pastels; teal blue; all greens, especially for career and money; pink for gentle friendship or tender, new love. White symbolizes the milky quality of the crescent moon and purity of intention.

Lady of the Hunt

In this spread, "project" means any creative endeavor or career/study plan. "Relationship" can be new love, coworkers, family, or friendships. You are the Lady of the Hunt and your question becomes your quest. If you have something specific in mind, ask your question while shuffling the cards. For example, *Tell me what I need to know about my new (love, work situation, and so on).* For more information about the layout in general, or a specific card, use the three-card spread described in chapter 2.

Breathe deeply and shuffle your tarot deck. When you are ready, lay the cards out in positions one through six, as shown in figure 3.

Position 1: This Begins Your Project or Relationship. Your life experience, and what you bring from the past into the new situation. What brought you to this moment?

Position 2: This Shapes Your Project or Relationship. Outside influences, significant events, other people that shape the situation.

Position 3: This Is At the Center of Your Project or Relationship. The main theme, lesson, opportunity, or challenge of the situation. *The focus card*—all other cards revolve around the center and it carries the most weight in the reading.

Position 4: This is What Your Project or Relationship Needs to Succeed. The effort you will make, the "elbow grease" required for your goals and ambitions to be realized, the follow-up to your magical workings on the physical plane.

Position 5: The Direction or Path of Your Project or Relationship. Where you are headed, the future outlook.

Position 6: Advice Card. What is the best course of action to take with this new project or relationship? What do you need to know now?

To complete the Maiden reading, you can meditate with the cards, write a journal entry, keep the cards on the altar until the next

Figure 3: Lady of the Hunt

waxing moon, or simply close. Carry a card or two with you during the day to strengthen the connection between you and your Maiden spirit's desire. Affirm your personal power to create your destiny: "I awaken to my own creative powers. This, or something better, is manifesting for me now, for the good of all, harming no one, according to free will. So must it be."

Lady of the Hunt Sample Reading

Sarah is a single mother in need of extra income. She works at a coffee shop and goes to college part-time, majoring in English. She can't afford more daycare, so she knows she has to supplement her income from home. Her English professor tells her she has a way with words, and Sarah loves to write. She begins thinking of ways to make money writing at home, but can't formulate a plan.

Sarah spends time browsing the writing and home-based business sections of her local bookstore. She discovers there are freelance opportunities in her own city, writing for small businesses, agencies, and charitable organizations. Sarah has never tried to "market" herself before, and she has doubts about whether she can do it. She knows her new project involves creativity, and realizes she must possess the confidence required to get started. Because Sarah doesn't know where to begin, she does a Lady of the Hunt layout for inspiration.

Position 1: Five of Pentacles. Sarah is focused on the survival issues of money, housing, job, and food because she is unable to support her daughter and go to school on her salary. She is filled with self-doubt. The Five of Pentacles tells her that financial aid is available if she swallows her pride and looks for it. Possibilities include a school loan and federal assistance for her child.

Position 2: Queen of Wands. The Queen of Wands suggests a businesswoman who gives good advice. Sarah searches the Yellow Pages and makes an appointment with a counselor at the Association of Women Business Owners. She plans to ask a lot of questions. She also plans to seek financial aid for college.

Position 3: Seven of Wands. Sarah knows that freelance writing is very competitive and it may be hard to break in to the field. She also knows she is a good writer and must stay determined if she is to succeed. The Seven of Wands suggests she needs to believe in her own abilities and strike out on her own. It validates her desire for self-employment but warns her that friends and family may "put her on the defensive" about the choices she is making.

Position 4: Eight of Pentacles. Elbow grease and concentration! The Eight of Pentacles suggests an apprenticeship and starting over in a new profession. Sarah's interest, enthusiasm, and willingness to learn about home-based freelance writing make up for her lack of experience.

She knows she will have to spend long hours doing a thorough market search, making cold calls to businesses, and sending out brochures if her project is to succeed. The suit of Pentacles tells her that she will make money, but not immediately. A training period will be required. The Eight, in particular, reminds Sarah that she will look unsettled to others as she builds her new career.

Position 5: The Sun. Sarah smiles when she sees the Sun. It tells her that she will succeed as a freelance writer. It also suggests that she needs to be playful. Sarah has been undecided about her "specialty area" of writing. She needs to decide upon a focus as she begins her market search. The Sun shows a child upon a horse and it dawns on her: begin the market search with organizations and agencies that focus on children's issues and care. The Sun tells her that she will have innovative ideas.

Position 6: The Six of Pentacles. Two things come to mind when Sarah draws the Six of Pentacles. First, she may have to volunteer her writing services for awhile to establish a reputation and gain experience. This card reminds Sarah to be generous with her writing skills in order to restore faith in her own ability to succeed.

Second, Sarah realizes she may have been overlooking financial assistance. The Five of Pentacles supports this idea in position one. The Six promises a financial backer. Sarah decides to ask the counselor at the Association of Women Business Owners about bank loans and financial assistance for start-up expenses. For inspiration, she leaves the layout on the altar until the next waxing moon. Sarah plans to do another Lady of the Hunt spread at that time. She carries the Fool with her during the day to remind her to trust the process as she embarks on her new career.

The Crone

The waning, or decreasing, moon represents the Crone Goddess. The Crone is the elder wisewoman, Grandmother Spider, acquainted with the night, decay, and death. She encompasses duality and holds dark and light, life and death, destruction and creation at the same time. She is called Hecate, Kali, Dana, Nemesis, and Rhiannon.

The Crone is past Her time of bleeding and is the Keeper of the Mysteries at the gateway to the Underworld. She can see past, present, and future at once and is the Goddess of Prophecy. She is the cauldron of death and rebirth. Her wisdom is helpful to women of *any* age. The Crone gives you the ability to put things in perspective and see the big picture. Her special children are elders, widows, people with life-threatening illnesses, victims of violent crimes, and all souls in pain.

The Crone offers strength and wisdom in the dark. She will not seek or call upon you. You must search for, and learn to trust, the darkness. Her gifts are wisdom, transformation, clairvoyance, protection, peaceful endings, and profound spiritual healing.

During the dark phase of the moon, call upon the Goddess of Retribution and Justice for protection against sexual harassment, domestic violence, and rape. Be certain your request is unselfish and justified. If it's not, you may find yourself being chased by Her vengeance. This Goddess, more than any other, believes in equal opportunity. She plays no favorites and does not respond kindly to malicious or frivolous requests.

All the Goddess archetypes are positive, but the Crone is often feared. Many books will advise you to stay away from magical workings during the dark phase of the moon. The Crone is misunderstood. After all, she became the ugly hag with warts who shows up on Halloween.

I suggest that the Crone offers new ways of exploring possibilities and new ways of interacting with the world. Rather than selecting "acceptable parts" of the Crone to work with, use Her entire energy. Instead of fragmenting and cutting yourself off from your nature, recognize that "all this is you." The Crone returns us to a state of integration and wholeness that encompasses the totality of our personalities—from birth to death to being reborn of the Mother.

Opinions differ, but I, for one, do not hesitate to practice magic at any phase of the moon. If my need is great—and my intent pure—I believe the Goddess is, above all, ready and willing to help Her children whenever they are in need, regardless of the moon's phase.

The Crone Ritual

The waning moon is a time for reflecting on the entire cycle of life, from beginnings to endings. The Crone is not a birth Goddess, but a teacher of the deepest of mysteries. Her powers concern harvesting, turning inward, wisdom, prophecy, setting explicit goals, changing priorities, strong protection, letting go, and seeing life against an eternal backdrop. The Crone is honored at Samhain and with the Maiden and Mother at Yule. Crone rituals offer strength or wisdom in the dark. Her gifts are transformation, clairvoyance, protection, peaceful endings, and spiritual healing.

Amethyst crystals, shale, slate, black coral, obsidian, onyx, diamonds, and silver or platinum jewelry add power to the Crone's altar. Objects and figurines symbolic of Crone's wisdom include apples, black cauldrons, claws set in silver, owls, ravens, serpents, spiders, and black cats.

Note: Onyx may cause depression in some, but it is a potent stone for those aligned to it, especially those with a strong Capricorn in their natal (birth) chart. Diamonds hold, absorb, magnify, and transmit pain; they retain impressions and are hard to clear. Positive diamonds transmit pure knowing and spirit, so use diamond only if it is particularly meaningful to you.

The Crone's Tarot Cards

The Crone's number is Nine and multiples of Nine. Nine symbolizes wisdom, magic, spiritual completion, and wholeness. In tarot, the Hermit, card 9, reflects Crone knowledge. His purpose is to assist people who are no longer where they were and are not yet where they hope to be. The Hermit is a midwife to the psyche: by turning within to find answers, the Hermit patiently guides us to the wisdom of our Higher Self.

The Hermit represents illumination of the inner world when the outer one is dark, and he gently urges us to go within to find our own answers. He teaches us of the need for solitude to find our inner strength. The Hermit understands the natural cycle of life, death, and rebirth. The Hermit's gifts are the gifts of the Crone: patience, acceptance, and profound understanding.

All the Nines in tarot show wisdom, growth, lessons learned, and completion through their suits: Nine of Wands, spiritual strength in reserve and wise use of power; Nine of Cups, wish fulfillment, emotional joy, and contentment; Nine of Swords, the promise of growth by coming to terms with one's problems; Nine of Pentacles, satisfaction and material benefits as a reward for effort.

The Moon, card 18, as a multiple of Nine, represents the Crone's deep mysteries and a time of spiritual wisdom and growth, but it comes with a price. We must be willing to experience the mystery, wonder, and terror of spiritual evolution. The shadow side must be recognized and integrated for growth to occur. The Moon symbolizes the magic and fear of meeting the unconscious in its uncontrolled aspects. The gift of the Moon's energy is wisdom.

The Scents of the Crone

Orchids are associated with the dark moon and the Crone. Vanilla is a byproduct of the orchid. Lilies symbolize death and rebirth. Any night-blooming flower, such as jasmine, or any heavy scent, including opium, neroli, black narcissus, myrrh, or musk is aligned with the Crone and Her mysteries. Sandalwood and frankincense are all-purpose scents, especially for protection.

Magical Brews of the Crone

Apples have represented knowledge since time began. In Celtic beliefs, spirits go to Avalon, or Land of the Apples. They are symbols of the soul. Apples signify death, rebirth, and wisdom. Use any apple-based magical brew including herbal tea, juice, and cider. Vanilla adds a delicious flavor and is attuned to the Crone.

Candles of the Crone

Black or dark burgundy is the color of night, shadows, mystery, and letting go. Black also absorbs negativity. If using a black candle, be sure to discard the candle when your ritual is complete, be it immediately or at the next dark moon. Purple symbolizes deep wisdom, strong protection, spirituality, and profound healing. White is associated with initiation, pure intention, spiritual knowledge, and psychic protection.

Dark Goddess

The Dark Goddess will not seek or call upon you. You must ask for Her help and guidance and then trust what you learn in the dark. Her gift is the ability to put your life in perspective and see the big picture. She can assist you in finding your place on the web of life and suggest future direction because She sees the past, present, and future at once. Cards one through three look at the past and tell you what you carry into the present. Cards four through six describe the present and how it can shape the future. Cards seven through nine offer suggestions for the future based on the action you take in your own behalf today.

Use the Dark Goddess spread to help you see the higher overview of your current situation. The cards will either represent a situation or give you advice about that situation. Pay special attention to any number Nine card in this spread, because the Dark Goddess wants to talk to you.

If you need more information from the layout in general, or about a specific card in the layout, use a three-card spread (found in chapter 2). Breathe deeply and shuffle your deck. If you have a specific question for the Crone, concentrate on it as you shuffle the entire deck. Lay the cards out in positions one through nine, as shown in figure 4. The cards reflect the decreasing moon through the magical number Nine.

Position 1: Protection. Indicates the area of your life where you give away your power—your "soft spot" that needs to be protected if you are to be strong. Decide whether the card depicts a situation or gives you advice about that situation.

Position 2: Patience. Shows where you need to take it easy and allow things to happen in their own natural cycle. If it describes a situation, it depicts a circumstance that you are trying to "force." Do a three-card spread for advice on how to develop the wisdom of patience.

Position 3: Acceptance. Closely related to position two. What events, people, or circumstances are you trying to control or influence? This card will tell you where you need to know the difference between what you can change and what you cannot change.

Position three may also make a strong statement about the free will of others. If it puzzles you, do a three-card spread for more information.

Position 4: Peaceful Endings. Related to the information you received from cards two and three: You develop patience, and learn what to accept and release in love. Sometimes, the wisest thing to do is to "disconnect" from the person or situation. Where do you need to let go of love so growth can occur? Is a ritual of mourning indicated?

Figure 4: Dark Goddess

Position 5: Clairvoyance. The Crone is the Goddess of Prophecy. How can you develop Her psychic gifts in your own life? This card will either show you where you need to concentrate your efforts on thought patterns that block or hinder your psychic development, or give you advice on how to nurture your psychic gifts.

Position 6: Perspective. This is the "ah-ha" card, the moment of stepping back to get the big picture so you can put your life in perspective with the "master plan." Look for the relationship between this card and the others in the spread. If this card is from the Major Arcana, do a three-card spread for more information. If you have a Trump Card in position six, you can be certain the Goddess wants to talk to you now.

Position 7: Spiritual Healing. This is your "inner work" card; it shows where you have been hurt and what needs to be healed for growth to occur. If this card is especially uncomfortable, it is because it's a graphic depiction of your own woundedness. Healing begins with awareness. Talk to a trusted friend or adviser about the situation if you find it particularly disturbing. Get help if you need it.

Position 8: Crone's Wisdom. The advice card. The cards in positions one through seven weave a story about your life. Every situation is related to every other circumstance—this becomes apparent if we can step back and see the higher overview. What advice does the Wisewoman Crone offer you?

Position 9: Transformation. The possible future. What are the gifts of the Crone that hide in the dark? If the card makes you uncomfortable, it may show the work that still needs to be done for transformation to occur. For example, let's say the Nine of Swords shows up here. Nine is the Crone's number. The key to liberation from mental anguish is confronting one's pain and fear. By embracing the shadow, the Crone offers you the freedom to live a full, joyful life.

To complete the Dark Goddess reading, you can meditate with the cards, write a journal entry, keep the cards on the altar until the next decreasing moon, or simply close. Carry a card or two with you during the day to strengthen the connection between you and the Dark Goddess. Affirm your personal power to transform your life: "I awaken to the wisdom of Crone and live my life without fear or limitation. This, or something better, is manifesting for me now, for the good of all, harming no one, according to free will. So must it be."

Sample Dark Goddess Reading

Elizabeth, or Liz, as her friends call her, is known in her coven as a healer and organizer, a high priestess, wisewoman crone. People are naturally attracted to her and she opens her home to all. She has an enclosed backyard and the neighbors either love her or leave her alone. For several years now, the coven has met in her home to celebrate the Sabbats and work magic at the full moon because she has the privacy to do so.

Elizabeth is pleased that the coven is an eclectic mix: Women of all ages, educational backgrounds, and economic circumstances are drawn to the mystery of the Goddess and the loving atmosphere of Elizabeth's home. She has to smile to herself because many prominent town citizens practice magic after dark. Elizabeth feels blessed that the women get along so well—until now.

She can't remember exactly when the bickering began, but it disturbs her to think the group may fall apart because of it. Attendance is down and people are taking sides, getting cliquish after Circle. Elizabeth works as a social worker/counselor during the day. Over the years she has learned that there are really only two kinds of conflicts: conflicts with people who are willing to work together to resolve the issue, and conflicts with people who escalate the issue. She is aware that group dynamics must be addressed if the coven is to survive and prosper.

Elizabeth wonders if she needs to suggest that the coven meet at other people's homes for a change, even though that means a loss of privacy and a ritual that is forced indoors. She also wonders if it's time to initiate another high priestess. Maybe she has been "boss" too long.

Elizabeth decides to call a special circle at the dark moon. The increasing negativity of the group upsets her and it is destroying the purpose of the coven. If an intervention isn't performed soon, the group will fall apart. She sends out invitations and clearly states the purpose of the dark moon ritual. She is both surprised and pleased that all coven members are in attendance. This gives her hope that they are concerned, too.

The coven agrees that after everyone has a chance to speak, the Guardian of Group Wisdom will summarize each card's significance. Elizabeth is chosen to be the Guardian because she has counseling experience and the layout is her idea. Elizabeth reminds the group that the purpose of the Dark Goddess spread for group wisdom is to determine what to release, what to keep and nurture, and which direction to take.

The coven invites the Crone into the circle and asks for Her wisdom and guidance. After ritual, but before the Circle is opened, Elizabeth shuffles the cards for a Dark Goddess reading. Each member present shuffles the cards in turn, asking that the information be for the good of all, harming no one. Elizabeth deals the nine-card Dark Goddess spread in the middle of the circle for all to see. The coven has decided to use a "talking piece" (a rattle passed around, in turn, to those who wish to speak). Only the member holding the rattle has the floor. Everyone then has an opportunity to discuss the personal meaning of the cards, in a respectful manner, as they relate to the dynamics of the troubled group.

Position 1: Five of Swords. The Five of Swords quickly defines the group's problem with communication. Someone is gossiping, and the Five suggests a power struggle between two dominant personalities. Georgia and Kaye are too much alike. Each wants to be the center of attention. Each is used to having her own way. Without realizing it, they have polarized the group. Whenever there is polarization caused by dominant personalities, all members of the group are affected.

Domination of one person over another can ruin any group. The Five of Swords reminds the group that there is always a choice: Does there have to be a winner or loser in this situation? This card asks that everyone turn away from the struggle. Pride must be swallowed and limitations accepted by everyone before progress can be made.

Position 2: Two of Cups, Reversed. The coven members agree that they have been trying to "force" Georgia and Kaye to get along.

The reversed Two of Cups suggests a need for emotional balance and cordial encounters, but the number of Wands and Swords in the spread indicates that patience is not a strong point of this group. The Two of Cups reminds the group to settle minor disputes before they get out of hand, without taking sides. It can also mean that Georgia and Kaye don't get along because they remind each other of a negative childhood experience.

Position 3: The Tower. The Tower is a wake-up call to be honest about beliefs and thinking patterns. It suggests that the group's structure is breaking apart for a reason: Like it or not, there is a need to break down existing group dynamics to make way for a new and better way of communicating. The overthrow of existing conditions brings new opportunities and a fresh start.

Everyone agrees that they have been trying to control the negative feelings in the group by ignoring them. In doing so, the power struggle only gets worse. The group cannot change the personality conflict between Kaye and Georgia, but the individual members can change the way they react to it by not taking sides. The Tower indicates that this breakdown in behavior is essential if the group is to grow and prosper.

Position 4: Seven of Wands. Position four is closely related to cards two and three: The Two of Cups reversed indicates the need for emotional balance, and the Tower suggests that emotional balance will be restored only when there is a breakdown in established ways of thinking and acting. In a group reading, the Seven of Wands suggests that the group is strong enough to survive conflict. The Seven is closely related to wisdom and knowledge, and promises the group that it can meet the challenges of conflict and rivalry—if the members can stand up to the dominant personalities. By now, the members of the group start to assess their individual contributions to the turmoil. They realize that what affects one, affects all, and it is time to let go of old behavior.

Position 5: Five of Wands. At first the group is puzzled. What can the Five of Wands have to do with psychic gifts? After passing the rattle a few times, it becomes clear: The Five of Wands is a card of action, rivalry, and competition, qualities that hinder the group's rapport. If the group is to grow spiritually, strengthening the connection to the Great Mother, then it must address the rivalry between the group members. There must be a balance of power between rival members before the group, as a whole, can become powerful.

Position 6: King of Swords. The King of Swords calls for fairness, diplomacy, tact, cooperation, and negotiation. He uses words rather than force, and is the King of Communication. This card's presence assures the group that they are on the right track, truly an "ah-ha" moment for its members.

The King of Swords reminds the group that the answers to their problems lie in recognizing the shadow side of his energy: The members must get in touch with their own tendencies to be selfish, sarcastic, aloof, aggressive, or suspicious. In doing so, they release a healing energy that communicates fairness and negotiation. They must be honest and say what they truly think and feel for growth to occur. The group realizes that the "master plan" of this particular conflict is to yield awareness of the shadow and its power. The number of Swords in this spread suggests that the primary issues involve resolving group conflict and making difficult decisions.

Position 7: Queen of Swords. The Queen of Swords has a spiritual depth caused by prolonged struggle. She can also be unforgiving, cold, and unsympathetic. Emotions have flared in this group. The number of Wands in the spread speaks of anger. Several women, including Kaye and Georgia, have joined the coven because they need to heal from their own woundedness.

Words can hurt or heal. The King of Swords in position six indicates that the shadow side of communication—using words that hurt—needs to be addressed. The Queen of Swords suggests to the group that spiritual healing will occur when the group takes a time-out from emotions in favor of introspection. The group agrees not to meet again until the next Sabbat, about six weeks later.

Position 8: Temperance. Temperance supports the coven's plan to halt meetings for awhile. The essence of this card is "easy does it, but do it." Moderation in all things. The group decides that, in an effort to bond, they have been too intense, meeting too often. They also know that resolution of the conflict is a test of some sort. The fact they all chose to attend the dark moon gathering shows that they are willing to be tested. Temperance asks the group to mix and match until they find what works.

Crone wisdom through Temperance suggests experimentation—holding the Sabbats and Esbats at different locations, passing around the leadership role, establishing guidelines, doing things differently for awhile until equilibrium is achieved. Temperance asks for patience in all things in a calm and relaxed atmosphere. It also calls for perseverance, compassion for one another, and forgiveness.

By focusing their attention on what the group needs—improved communication skills and anger management—the coven members are promised renewed energy and a sense of harmony.

Position 9: Three of Cups. In a phrase, a time to celebrate. The Three of Cups is often used as a timing card because of its association with holidays. It confirms the group's decision to wait until the next Sabbat to reconvene. The Three of Cups offers a time of joy. The reward for resolution of the power struggle between dominant members is great: Confusion in relationships is lifted, estrangements are mended, old wounds heal, and the group can move forward. By doing the hard work of conflict resolution, group interactions with people of like minds leads to spiritual awakening. Through shared ceremony and ritual, the coven will experience an inner peace and reverence for the Goddess.

The ability to maintain the group is based on its ability to communicate without shame or blame, pulling out of polarity and seeing the underlying issues. The coven needs to trust that all members are willing to preserve the integrity of what they have created, to see the process through to completion. Yes, some members may leave, but it will be by choice, not coercion.

The coven found that preconflict bonding had been sweet, but not as potent as postconflict bonding. The Circle has lost its illusions by coming through a crisis together. Conflict resolution is scary as they learn to speak their truths, but they will be a more powerful group because of it.

4

The Cycling of Time: Darkness Into Light

The holidays exist whether we recognize them or not.

—VICKI NOBLE

Samhain: October 31

We begin the Wheel of the Year with Samhain, also known as November Eve, Feast of the Dead, Festival of the Apples, All Hallows Eve, and, of course, Halloween. Samhain [sow'-en] is an old Celtic word meaning "summer's end,"[1] and is considered the witch's New Year.

During Samhain festivities, huge bonfires were constructed and lit for a week to mark the death of summer and the birth of winter. Samhain was the night of death in a time when the passage of the dead was greatly revered. It was a time for pagan people to honor their ancestors, deceased loved ones, and all those who had gone before.

The people gave thanks to their departed loved ones and believed the dead still helped them from the spirit world. The bonfires marked the end of summer and led the way for the dead, as their spirits journeyed to a higher realm called Summerland. The modern Roman Catholic Church observes of All Saints' Day

(November 1) and All Souls' Day (November 2), which originate from this pagan reverence for the dead.

Apples were the fruit of immortality and were buried on Samhain so the souls returning to the mortal world in spring would have enough to eat during the harsh winter months. Because of this custom, Samhain is called the Festival (or Feast) of Apples.

On the night of Samhain, the veil, or separation, between the physical and spiritual worlds is thinnest. The tradition of carving dreadful faces on hollowed-out pumpkins and then placing a lit candle inside stems from the belief that the souls of the dead walk abroad on Samhain night. These pumpkins, or jack-o'-lanterns, were placed about to frighten away unwelcome, or malevolent, spirits.

Pagans believed that unwelcome spirits could wreck havoc at a moment's notice. Children dressed up in dark costumes and went about shouting "Trick-or-Treat!" It was considered bad luck not to offer a treat. The modern custom of trick-or-treating also has origins in England, where the poor went from house to house on All Hallows Eve begging for soul cakes or money. Whether "beggars' night" or chasing away unwelcome spirits, the custom of knocking on doors at Halloween most certainly has its roots in pagan tradition.

In present time, witches say a temporary farewell to the God at Samhain. As he dies, he readies himself to be reborn of the Goddess at Yule. Samhain is a time of reflection, letting go, looking back over the year, and coming to terms with things over which we have no control. It is a time to understand that through death in winter we pass on to new life in spring. We release the old, listen to inner wisdom, and await the new.

Casting spells of protection, and neutralizing harm can be practiced at any time of the year, but it is especially appropriate at Samhain. Because the veil between the worlds is thinnest, all forms of divination are most powerful, including the use of tarot cards. Please refer to chapter 2 for basic information about ritual design.

The Samhain Ritual

Samhain is a time for releasing worn-out ideas, relationships, and habits in order to make way for the new. It is a perfect time for listening to inner wisdom, protecting all living creatures, and neutralizing harm.

To enhance Samhain energies, amethyst, smoky quartz, obsidian, ruby, or any dark stone can be worn as jewelry or placed upon the altar. After deciding on your magical working(s) for the Samhain season, focus your intention to realize your desire. (*Note:* Use caution when working with onyx. It can cause depression in some people. It has the most positive effect on those with a strong Capricorn in their birth chart.)

Samhain Tarot Cards

Place the Death card, card 13, on your altar to symbolize your intention to let go of worn-out ideas or habits. The Hermit, card 9, represents going within to find your own wise counsel.

The Scents of Samhain

Apple, pumpkin, vanilla, sage, or the scent of any autumn flower such as marigold. If incense smoke bothers you, try heating oil in a fireproof burner, or simply hold an apple in your hand and partake of its magical aroma.

Magical Brews of Samhain

Apple tea, of course, or nettle; mulled cider or wine with spices such as cinnamon and cloves. Any pungent, spicy herbal infusion that reminds you of autumn. Vanilla is especially attuned to the Dark Goddess and adds a delightful flavor to your magical brew.

Samhain Candles

Samhain is a time for releasing and letting go, a time to look inward for wisdom. Use black or deep burgundy candles for releasing, and purple for inner wisdom. Orange attracts that which you desire.

Fruit of Wisdom Tarot Layout

The apple is sacred to witches. If you cut an apple horizontally in half, it reveals a five-pointed star called a pentagram. The pentagram is not related to the Christian devil because witches do not believe in any devil; this association with evil is an aberration of Christianity and has nothing whatsoever to do with witchcraft.

The pentagram is a beautiful star, and stars provide light as we navigate the darkness. The five points of the pentagram symbolize Earth, Air, Fire, Water, and Spirit. Its enveloping circle means the endless cycle of life, death, and rebirth. Pentagrams are associated with the feminine and are powerful for protection.

Cut an apple in half horizontally to reveal the pentagram. Contemplate this beautiful star as you shuffle and cut the tarot deck. When you are ready, place six cards in positions one through six, as shown in figure 5. If you need more information on a specific card, or the layout itself, do a three-card reading (described in chapter 2).

Position 1: A Time of Reflection. Fears and Blocks. What is holding you back from creating the life you want? What blocks you from your desires?

Position 2: Acceptance. Who or what do you need to accept? What cannot be changed?

Position 3: Release and Let Go. What is no longer useful to you? What habits, relationships, or thought patterns are worn out?

Position 4: Keep, Nurture, and Protect. What talents, skills, and abilities do you need to keep and nurture? What do you need to protect?

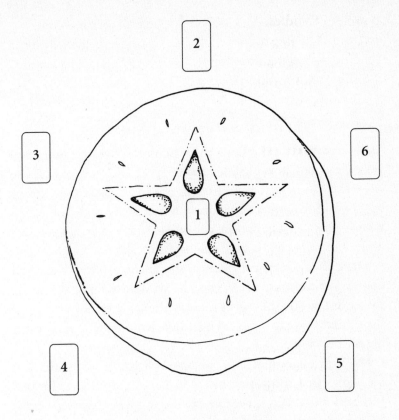

Figure 5: Fruit of Wisdom

Position 5: Crone's Wisdom. **What is your intuition telling you? What can you learn from your situation?**

Position 6: Cauldron of Rebirth. Awaiting the New. **What future are you building as a result of reflecting, accepting, releasing, nurturing, and protecting?**

To complete the Samhain reading, you can meditate with the cards, write a journal entry, keep the cards on the altar until Yule, or simply close. Carry a card or two with you during the day to strengthen the connection between you and inner wisdom. Affirm your personal power to protect all that you love: "I awaken to the Samhain season and release all that is holding me back from fulfilling my spirit's desire. This, or something better, is manifesting for me now, for the good of all, harming no one, according to free will. So must it be."

Samhain Reading Sample

Marie has worked at a large chain bookstore for two years, but feels she is now overqualified for the post. The job was perfect while she was in school, and she hoped to get a management or buyer position upon graduation; however, she recently completed a Bachelor of Arts degree in Liberal Studies, and hasn't gotten a promotion. Now, as a college graduate, she can't find employment.

Marie is discouraged because she spent a lot of time and money working hard for the degree. While she enjoys her work, the pay is low and she yearns for something better. She wonders if she should move to a larger city, where employment opportunities are better.

Marie loves autumn, and Samhain is her favorite holiday, but she senses that something inside of herself is blocking her full potential. What can it be? She decides to take advantage of this magical time of year, and does a Fruit of Wisdom layout to determine why she feels restless and discouraged.

Position 1: Nine of Swords. Marie knows she has anxiety about finding gainful employment as a college graduate. All her friends tell her she will be a success, but she doubts herself. The Nine of Swords suggests that, however unfounded her feelings of impending doom are, the pain is very real. Marie is caught in a spiral of disappointment and disillusion, which deepens her feelings of depression. The more depressed she feels, the more she's disappointed. And so the spiral feeds on itself.

The Nine of Swords indicates that Marie does not know the true source of her feelings of sorrow. This card means that even though the current situation is difficult, it's not as bad as she thinks. If Marie feels she can't get through this alone, she needs to seek counseling, see an adviser, or talk to a friend about how she's feeling. When Marie confronts her pain head-on, she will overcome it.

Position 2: The Hierophant. At first Marie is unsure of what the Hierophant card is trying to tell her. She meditates, writes in her journal, and looks through her tarot books. Slowly, the meaning becomes clear: She needs to accept that her workplace has an established order and way of promoting its employees from within. Marie has been impatient about advancing to a management or buyer position. The Hierophant reminds her that the business world has an established way of doing things and there isn't much she can do to hurry the process.

The Hierophant's message is clear: If she wants to advance in a large organization, success comes from following the rules, aligning herself to the powers that be, and waiting her turn. But the Hierophant also reminds Marie not to compromise her personal integrity in the process.

Position 3: Two of Swords. The Two of Swords in this position reinforces the doubt and worry found in position one. Marie has reached a fork in the road. The time has come to make a decision: wait for a management position at her current worksite and be content to do so, or seek employment in another city.

The Two of Swords reminds Marie that the results aren't in yet. She needs to be patient and let go of her nagging fear of failure. The card suggests that once she makes a decision between waiting or moving on, her life will resume its forward motion.

Position 4: The Magician. Marie knows that doubt and worry have resulted in feelings of powerlessness to change her situation. The Magician urges her to visualize a goal and get to work; the time has come to roll up her sleeves. Marie can nurture and protect her self-esteem by taking action on her own behalf.

She has been passive at work and realizes she has been waiting for someone to notice her. She hasn't even made it clear to the human resources department that she is interested in advancement. Marie just assumed that "someone" would notice her once she had her college degree. She decides to redo her resumé and apply for the position she wants. By doing so, she sets a powerful creative force in motion.

The Magician works on all levels of existence. Marie chooses to take care of the mundane level but knows she needs to work on the esoteric level, as well. She plans to visualize her ideal job on a daily basis, for the good of all, its equivalent or better, harming no one. She will also place her resumé and the bookstore's business card next to the Magician on her altar.

While she visualizes, she will light orange and green candles and burn cinnamon incense to attract the perfect job and financial success. Marie already feels the force of the Magician's energy, but she knows she needs to act now. The fiery Magician's motivation can soon wane if not supported by real action on a regular basis. Marie makes a note to do a Lady of the Hunt layout on the next increasing moon.

Position 5: Wheel of Fortune. This card provides Marie with her "ah-ha" moment: The Wheel of Fortune reveals her connection to luck and destiny. She is astonished to realize that fear of failure has kept her from asking for the advancement. What if they say no?

The card tells her that she doesn't have to remain locked in the status quo. Coupled with the Magician, the Wheel of Fortune means that if Marie takes the risk of actually making her wishes for advancement known (and directly faces the possibility of failure), luck will ride with her. Once she sets everything in motion, the universe will respond to her desires. Fear of failure has been holding her back. Taking a risk opens new doors, and Marie will create her own destiny.

Position 6: Ace of Pentacles. The Ace of Pentacles promises positive rewards for hard work. It stands for prosperity and success down the road. The Ace assures Marie that her application for advancement will be successful if she has the patience to wait for it. She's in the right place at the right time to set good things in motion. When placed with the Magician and Wheel of Fortune, Marie knows that she has the power to manifest her plans and dreams; in short, to create her own destiny. She decides to leave the layout on her altar until the next new moon.

Yule: December 21 or 22 (Winter Solstice)

On Yule, witches honor the Goddess for giving birth to a son, the God. The Goddess draws light into her womb during the darkest time of the year, from Samhain to Yule. She gives birth to the light, her son the God, at the winter solstice. Because ancient pagans honored divine birth at Yule, it is no accident that Christians chose December 25 as the birthday of their own divine son.

Since the God is symbolized by the sun, the winter solstice (also known as "the birth of light") marks the point of the year when the sun is reborn as well. In the Northern Hemisphere, the winter solstice falls on December 21 or 22, when the sun seems to stand still at its most southeastern point over the Tropic of Capricorn. This is the longest night and shortest day of the year, after which daylight hours grow longer. From this point on, the sun rises a little earlier, giving more light to the cold days of winter.

This is a time of balance and a time of change. "Yule" is the Anglo-Saxon word for the winter solstice, and is derived from the Nordic word *iul,* meaning "wheel," related to the sacred circle or wheel of nature.[2] In an agricultural society, survival meant having enough food. The Yule ritual symbolically hurried the end of a harsh winter to celebrate the bounty of spring, when food was once again plentiful.

Yule was the day when Druids honored the battle between the Holly King and the Oak King by cutting the sacred mistletoe from the oak tree and letting it fall to the ground. The Holly King has symbolized the death and darkness since Samhain; at Yule, the Oak King, who represents light and life, defeats the Holly King.

Great fires were lit to celebrate the return of the sun. The act of burning a Yule log at Christmas is a surviving remnant of that Druid custom, but also shares a relationship with the entire Season of Light—Chanukah, Kwanza, and St. Lucia's Day are but three life-affirming holidays during the darkest time of year. Long ago, pagans brought fir trees, holly, ivy, and pine boughs into their homes at Yule as a reminder of returning light and life. The Christian customs of displaying Christmas trees and decorating with evergreens are directly related to this Yule tradition.

In present time, the Goddess gives birth to the God at Yule, and witches are reminded that birth is a continuance of life, not its beginning, and the ultimate result of death is rebirth. It is a time for balancing our nature, spirit, and physical body. Meditations focus on the hidden energies lying dormant within the earth and ourselves during winter. It is also a time of returning hope, and witches gather to celebrate and make merry. Children receive gifts from Father Winter, homes are decorated, and good food abounds. Yule reminds us to take care of each other, the earth, and all her creatures in the gentle, kind, and magical season of goodwill.

The Yule Ritual

Yule is the season for peace, returning hope, and restoring balance. It is the perfect time for planning, making wishes, and seeking visions. When worn or placed upon the altar, clear quartz crystals, garnet, ruby, and green tourmaline will enhance the energies of Yule. After deciding on your magical working(s) for the Yule season, focus your intention to realize your desire.

Yule Tarot Cards

Place the Star, card 17, on your altar as a sign of returning hope. Justice, card 11, restores balance, while the Sun, card 19, symbolizes the hidden energies lying dormant in the winter, and welcomes the return of the God. Use the Nine of Cups for making wishes and the Two of Wands for seeking a vision.

The Scents of Yule

Pine, cedar, balsam, fir, cinnamon, clove, mistletoe, orange, frankincense, myrrh, rosemary, bay, and juniper all add atmosphere, beauty, and depth to your winter solstice celebrations.

Magical Brews of Yule

Wassail; hibiscus, cranberry, apple, orange, or ginger tea; mulled cider or red wine with spices such as cinnamon and clove.

Candles of Yule

Set a large red candle in a bowl or cauldron to symbolize the birth of the sun. Green represents life, ever present and renewable, gold for sunlight, and white for the purity of new fallen snow.

Solstice Light

In the darkest of seasons, the Yule sun begins to rise a little earlier each day, and all the world seems ready for change. Use the Solstice Light spread to strengthen your hopes for the future. Plan, make wishes, raise your spirits—knowing that the creative fire of spring is promised to you at Yule.

If you have a specific question in mind, ask it as you shuffle the cards. For more information about the Solstice Light layout, or a specific card in the layout, use one of the three-card spreads in chapter 2.

To begin, shuffle the cards and place them in positions one through six, as shown in figure 6.

Position 1: Returning Hope. What are you hopeful about? If this card feels negative to you, it depicts painful issues that will be resolved or healed in the coming year. Remember, *all* cards show a spectrum of life, from happy to sad, and offer opportunities to learn wisdom.

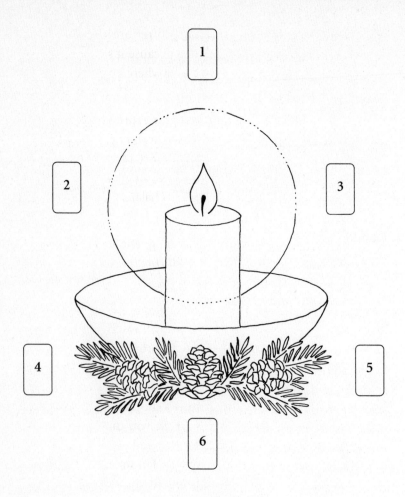

Figure 6: Solstice Light

Position 2: Making Wishes. What does your heart desire? Again, if you don't like the card, it is because it depicts an uncomfortable situation that you wish were different.

Position 3: Seeking Visions. What is your vision for the future? Where do you see yourself next year at this time? Do a three-card timeline reading from chapter 2 if you need to clarify the meaning of position three.

Position 4: Sense of Balance. What will restore balance to your life? If the card feels negative, it is because it shows an area of your life that is out of balance and where you need to focus your efforts to restore order.

Position 5: Goodwill Toward Others. Your expression of love. Yule is the season of giving. In what way can you open your heart to others? If this card makes you uncomfortable, it indicates a situation in need of repair, forgiveness, or making an amend. Note whether card four, your sense of balance, is related to card five, goodwill toward others.

Position 6: Advice. The next step. Planning. The action card. What can you do on the mundane level during the winter months to make your hopes and wishes real?

Look at cards one through five: your hopes, wishes, vision for the future, sense of balance, and goodwill toward others. What story do they weave together to advise you on your next course of action?

To complete the Yule reading, you can meditate with the cards, write a journal entry, keep the cards on the altar until Imbolc, or simply close. Carry a card or two with you during the day to strengthen the connection between you and your vision for the future. Affirm your personal power to plan the life you want: "I awaken to the season of Yule and bring my spirit's desire into balance. This, or something better, is manifesting for me now, for the good of all, harming no one, according to free will. So must it be."

Sample Yule Reading

Lauren is not looking forward to the Yule season. She is between relationships—again. The sparkle and sounds of the season do not match the heaviness she feels in her heart. Of course, her family expects her home for the holidays, but she would rather not go. Lauren knows her parents love her, but she's weary of explaining her existence to them. Always the same old questions: *When will you go back to college and make something of yourself? What about your career?*

Lauren has hopes, dreams, and desires like any other young woman her age. But she feels adrift right now, losing focus of her heart's desire. She decides to do a Solstice Light reading to gain clarity at this special time of year. The first thing she notices about the spread is that it has four Cups in it. The dominance of Cups tells her that heart heaviness is on the emotional plane. She will be looking at descriptions of her feelings and what to do about those feelings.

Position 1: Five of Cups. Lauren doesn't feel hopeful when she looks at this card. She realizes it shows painful issues that need healing in the coming year. She is still grieving her recent breakup, and the Five of Cups shows her disappointment. Lauren also knows that past family hurts are yet to be resolved. Is that why she doesn't want to go home for the holidays? In position one, the Five of Cups tells her that she needs to examine her situation(s) to see what she can learn before she moves on.

Position 2: The Empress. Lauren's desire is to have an abundant life. She can't tell her career-oriented parents that her heart's desire is to be a mother. All the women in her family have careers, and children come later in life. Her own sister is in law school. Lauren's ambitions take another path: She wants to have a life-partner and to nurture children now. Lauren knows it sounds old-fashioned and contrary to her family's plans for her, but motherhood is her deepest desire. She cherishes her power to create life.

Position 3: Ten of Cups. Lauren's vision for the future is to have a happy home. She sees herself feeling safe and secure, with real happiness, not just the absence of pain. Because she cannot fathom having this one year from now, she decides to do a three-card timeline spread at the end of the reading.

Position 4: Three of Cups. Lauren knows that she has been drinking too much since the breakup with her last partner. The

Three of Cups often means a time of celebration, but because it is in position four, it reminds Lauren to cut down on her indulgences. She realizes she hasn't been taking very good care of herself lately, and the Three of Cups tells Lauren where to focus her efforts to restore order to her life.

Position 5: Six of Cups. In the season of goodwill, Lauren's power to heal is in forgotten skills and old dreams. She used to be great with kids and dreamed of operating a daycare one day. The Six of Cups is about nostalgic memories and new opportunities. Children are also highlighted with this card. Lauren decides that the best way to activate the energy of the Empress (position two: making wishes) is to volunteer at the orphanage or Children's Hospital during the holiday season. What better way to open her heart to love in the season of goodwill?

Position 6: Ace of Cups. After Lauren looks at her story in cards one through five, she knows she has the power to create if she moves on from past disappointments and restores a sense of emotional balance to her life. The key to her happiness lies in opening her heart to children and nurturing others while being true to herself. The Ace of Cups tells Lauren that meditation will help open her heart chakra to new opportunities for love that will connect her to something larger than herself. She decides to learn all she can about meditation and practice it during the long winter months. Lauren is still in conflict over career versus family. The Ace of Cups reminds her that in conflicts between heart and mind, all is well if she follows her heart.

Sample Three-Card Timeline Reading

Lauren wants more information about the Ten of Cups in position three. She can't tell if a happy home a year from now is reality or fantasy, so she does a three-card timeline reading from chapter 2.

Card 1: Ten of Swords, Reversed. The reversed Ten of Swords tells Lauren that she needs to completely let go of a painful situation for new growth to occur. This is a card of great loss, and Lauren allows herself to cry for the first time when she sees it. The end of her relationship has been more painful than she has been willing to admit, and it is time to feel sad and grieve. She knows she is in the process of coming to terms with what is. The promise of the Ten of Swords is the ability to see things realistically and get on with broader issues and growth.

Card 2: Four of Swords. Time out. Between the stress of the holidays and the emotional turmoil of her breakup, Lauren knows it is time to heal and renew herself. The Four of Swords indicates that Lauren will take the time to rest during the winter months and turn within for guidance. The Ace of Cups in position six supports this timing because of her decision to meditate on a regular basis. The promise of the Four of Swords is calm after the storm.

Card 3: The Hanged Man. At first Lauren doesn't see a connection between having a happy home and the Hanged Man, so she journals about it and leaves the card on the altar for meditation. Then it hits her—in order to have a happy home, she will need to look at things differently, from another angle. Perhaps she has been defining "happy home" too rigidly. There are other ways to nurture and feel complete, especially with the Empress in position two of the solstice reading.

In the position of the far future, the Hanged Man is telling Lauren to question old beliefs and ideas to gain a deeper understanding of her life. Events in Lauren's life will force her to look within. The Four of Swords, as the near future, indicates she will spend time alone, something she has been afraid to do until now. She will have to sacrifice negative beliefs about herself and her circumstances.

The gift of the Hanged Man is seeing that the inner reality creates the outer reality. In a year's time, Lauren will know that happiness is an inside job. By making herself more loving, as indicated by the Ace of Cups in position six of the solstice reading, Lauren will have her happy home—whether with someone or alone.

Imbolc: February 2

In the Northern Hemisphere, February has a stark and bitter winter mood. The coldest weather and strongest blizzards await us. The icy frost lies just outside our doors, so we make ourselves content with home and indoor activities. At first glance, there is a springlike quality about Imbolc that feels out of sync with the harsh realities of winter.

Imbolc, meaning "ewe's milk," marks the beginning of a new life cycle, when snowdrop flowers first appear. It symbolizes purity, innocence, and freshness. Imbolc marks the recovery of the Goddess after giving birth to the God at Yule. The God is young, but his power is felt in the longer days. The warmth of the sun (the God) causes seeds to germinate and sprout.

Imbolc is also known as Candlemas (or Festival of Lights) and Feast of Brighid. Brighid, or Bride of Ireland, is the patron Goddess of Imbolc, good harvests, healthy babies, lactation, and women. She was an important Goddess to early Irish women and was known as Brid [breed], Brigid, Brigit, or Bride. Her hold over the Irish people was so great that the Christian church made her a saint, but she kept the greatest following among Irish women as their pagan Goddess.

At Imbolc, Brid represents the Goddess in Her Maiden aspect. She wears a crown of candles and is Goddess of fire and fertility. She is healer, protector, and Goddess of creative inspiration. The promise of spring has begun through the final days of winter.

Modern witches celebrate Imbolc as a Sabbat of purification after the shut-in life of winter. It is a festival of light and represents illumination and inspiration, a time for making plans and renewing strength. At Imbolc, witches visualize for creativity and renewed energy. Just beneath the crusted snow, budding new life waits for spring.

The Imbolc Ritual

Imbolc is a season of rest and introspection, preparing us for the creative fire of spring. The frantic pace of the outside world assumes less importance. During the quiet beauty of a snowy evening, we have the time for meditation and ritual, contemplation and planning. As the sun grows stronger every day, Imbolc reminds us that everything is born, dies, and is born again of the Mother. Because we are open to new ways of understanding, nature's barren time gives us the freedom to begin a process of deep healing.

Clear and rose quartz, hematite, lodestone, garnet, or citrine will enhance the energies of Imbolc when worn, carried, or placed upon the altar. After deciding your magical working(s) for Imbolc, focus your intention to realize your desire.

Imbolc Tarot Cards

Temperance, card 14, is called the Healing Angel. Place Temperance on your altar for all forms of healing and protection. Strength (card 8 or 11, depending on your deck) represents a balance between your physical and spiritual desires. Listening to your intuition during the quiet time of Imbolc strengthens you for the busier months ahead. The Ace or Queen of Wands radiates the energy of creative inspiration.

The Scents of Imbolc

Imbolc is the time of returning sunlight despite the cold. New life is stirring beneath the snow. Any scent that speaks to you of fire, creation, budding sexuality, strength, protection, or healing is appropriate. Favorite scents for this time of year include rosemary, frankincense, musk, and cinnamon.

Magical Brews of Imbolc

Spicy and full-bodied brews, especially those with cinnamon, honor the sun. Sage, chamomile, and rose hip teas are appropriate.

Imbolc marks the festival of the first calving, the time when cows give birth to their young. Pagans considered milk to be the fluid of life, and Brid is Goddess of Lactation. If you like the taste, add milk and honey to your tea, or simply add lemon.

Candles of Imbolc

Brid is in Her Maiden aspect and white is the color of the Maiden. Put as many white candles on the Imbolc altar as you can, because the candles' glow symbolizes the growing light. Pale blue represents crystalline snowflakes, and orange attracts the sun.

Brid's Wheel

February can be the harshest winter month, yet just beneath the snow, new life grows. Celebrate growth and new beginnings. Use the Brid's Wheel spread to make plans, gain strength, heal, and attain creative inspiration. Weave together your heart's desire on the last snowflake of winter, and await the promise of spring.

If you have a specific question in mind, ask your question as you shuffle the cards. For more information about Brid's Wheel, or a specific card in the layout, use one of the three-card spreads found in chapter 2.

When you are ready, place your cards in positions one through six, as shown in figure 7.

Position 1: Strength. This card shows where you are strong. If you don't like this card, it may be because it describes a painful life experience that has made you strong—or *will* make you strong if you directly face the issue.

Position 2: Heart's Desire. Your deepest desire. What do you really want? This card may surprise you. Do you dare to speak of your secret dreams?

Position 3: Healer. What needs to be healed if you are to be strong? Note whether or not there is a relationship between position one (strength) and this card. Does this card describe a situation or give you advice about a situation?

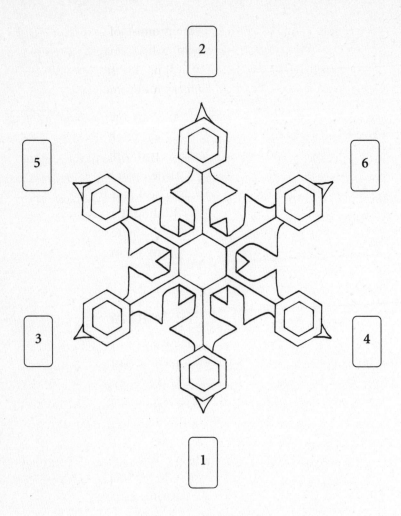

Figure 7: Brid's Wheel

Position 4: Creative Inspiration. When healing energy is released, creative inspiration is the result. What are you inspired to do? What creative activity fires you up?

Position 5: Making Plans. Based on the creative information of position four, what plans can you now make? Look for the relationships between cards three, four, and five: Healing energy produces a creative spark that needs planning to become real.

Position 6: New Growth. What is the promise of spring that lies just beneath the snow? By knowing where you are strong and focusing on your heart's desire, healing releases a creative fire that offers new beginnings. What is your promise of spring?

To complete the Imbolc reading, you can meditate with the cards, write a journal entry, keep the cards on the altar until Ostara, or simply close. Carry a card or two with you during the day to strengthen the connection between you and your heart's desire. Affirm your personal power to heal and grow strong: "I awaken to my strength of creative healing. I make plans and await the fire of spring. This, or something better, is manifesting for me now, for the good of all, harming no one, according to free will. So must it be."

Brid's Wheel Sample Reading

Audry works part-time at a small new age shop specializing in books and gifts. She supplements her income by giving tarot readings at the store. Not far away, a big chain bookseller recently opened, and it has a good metaphysical section. Since the national chain store is closer to the highway, thus more accessible, the new age shop has been losing business.

The energy at the small store is heavy. The winter has been long and hard and everyone is worried that the giftshop/bookstore will close. Audry struggles with chronic gastritis, and knows that worrying is not good for her. Her stomach seems to be her organ of stress, and lately she has been in a lot of pain after meals. The store's employees have done spells for protection and prosperity, but Audry realizes she must prepare herself for the grim possibility of closure. She decides to do a Brid's Wheel reading for insight into her situation.

Audry notices that three of the six cards are Wands. She also has a Sword, a Pentacle, and a Cup. This tells her that the cards are about creative inspiration, communication, and finding work that is emotionally satisfying. Audry loves computers, and computers

have crystals in them. She sees the dominance of Wands in her layout as a sign she should consider working with computers in some
way—but how?

Position 1: Queen of Swords. The Queen of Swords describes
someone who has loved and lost and lived to love again. This
Queen has known sorrow and survived. She combines feminin-
ity with creative intelligence and idealism. She is also the queen
of the written word. Audry knows that the Queen of Swords
describes her own life experiences. She has faced many difficul-
ties and has a strong sense of who she is because of it.

Position 2: King of Cups. The King of Cups is the emotional counselor of tarot. He heals himself by healing others, and he trusts
his intuition. Audry loves to help people gain insight into their
lives through the tarot. She prides herself on her ability to
counsel clients with a detached awareness. Audry's deepest
desire is to build a full-time tarot consultation service.

Position 3: Ten of Wands. Audry can't say no to the store manager.
Because of decreased business, staff has been cut and there is
pressure to work overtime without pay. Her manager has held
Audry emotionally hostage for quite awhile, indicating that
Audry should be grateful she still has a job. The manager has
even increased the percentage of the store's "cut" when Audry
does a tarot reading on the premises.

Audry knows that the Ten of Wands describes her inability
to say no to the store manager. She takes on too much, then
becomes angry with herself for doing so. Audry suddenly realizes that she is directing the anger at herself, and this accounts
for the stomach pains after eating. Her self-imposed burden of
singlehandedly saving the store is overshadowing her health.
The Ten of Wands suggests too much fire, but there is an
opportunity to release and transform. She needs to carry out
her responsibilities, but not deprive others of theirs. Audry
decides to stop working overtime without pay.

Position 4: Ace of Wands. The Ten of Wands in position three (healer) tells her that she is drained, tired, and angry right now, and has no energy to be creative. If Audry can release her self-imposed burden of singlehandedly trying to save the store, she will have the energy to be creative.

The Ace of Wands promises new endeavors. Again, Audry thinks of computers when she sees this card. She is inspired to develop a tarot consultation service in cyberspace. She decides to do a web search to see how other sites handle online psychic, astrological, and tarot readings. The very thought of this creative pursuit inspires Audry to find out more about it. Her head is spinning with new ideas. The Ace of Wands suggests Audrey is ready to strike out on her own in pursuit of a dream.

Position 5: Two of Wands. Because of the strong sense of self portrayed by the Queen of Swords in position one, Audry knows that she is a capable person. By releasing the burden of a failing store (Ten of Wands in position three), she has the time and energy to make plans.

The Two of Wands suggests collaboration with another person on a creative project. Audry makes a note to find out more about website design. With careful research, the card implies she will make the right connections at the right time. Audry senses that she is moving in the right direction with her plans for establishing an online tarot consultation service, but realizes there is much work ahead of her.

Position 6: Nine of Pentacles. Audry has long disliked feeling dependent upon a manipulative store manager for her livelihood. The Nine of Pentacles suggests a financially secure woman who works alone for the good of all. Audry's promise of spring is a new, independent, and creative way to do what she loves best: helping people by using her counseling and tarot skills.

Ostara: March 21
(Spring or Vernal Equinox)

The vernal, or youthful, equinox is the dramatic moment when the sun has reached the equator and the hours of day and night are equal everywhere on earth. It is the first day of true spring. The God is growing to maturity and rejoices in the abundance of nature. From this moment on, the hours of daylight lengthen until the Sun God reaches his peak of power at the summer solstice in June. Together, the Goddess and God inspire all living things to reproduce.

Ostara, sometimes called Eostre, is a Teutonic Goddess of Rebirth and is invoked on this day. Her symbols are flowers, rabbits, vines, and eggs that represent new life. East, the direction of new light, is derived from the name of the Goddess of Spring. For this reason, many witches face their altars east during the spring equinox.

The energies of the earth are awakening and we begin to act on all that we planned during Samhain, Yule, and Imbolc. It is a time of beginnings and planting spells for good fortune. If it is too cold to actually plant seeds during the spring equinox, tending a ritual garden until Beltane symbolizes the God's increasing power.

Ostara Ritual

Ostara, or the spring equinox, is the season of planting ideas for careers, relationships, and love. It is the perfect time to project for good health and good fortune. The promise of spring embraces change and new growth. Because we hold on to emotional debris, Ostara is a wonderful time to perform a spiritual housecleaning.

When worn or placed upon the altar, lapis lazuli, clear quartz crystal, garnet, agate, and rose quartz will enhance the energies of Ostara. After deciding your magical working(s) for Ostara, focus your intention to realize your desire.

Ostara Tarot Cards

Place the Chariot, card 7, on your altar as a sign of confidence in your ability to test what you have learned during the winter months. Unlike the Fool, the Chariot knows the reason for his journey and creates his own destiny through his actions. The Eight of Wands generates creative new ways forward. The Magician, card 1, symbolizes the ability to visualize goals on the physical, emotional, psychological, and spiritual planes of existence. He then asks you to *get to work* on those goals to make them your reality.

The Scents of Ostara

Spring is bursting forth with delicate new life. The scents of spring include tulips, daffodils, lavender, lilac, violet, jonquil, lily of the valley, and honeysuckle.

Magical Brews of Ostara

Crystal clear spring water; peach, rosebud, or vervain tea. Flavor your magical brews with honey, lemon, milk, or almond extract, if you like.

Candles of Ostara

Spring is a time of delicate beauty. All pastels are appropriate: green for new growth, pink for budding relationships, sky blue for spiritual housecleaning, white for purity of intention. Use your intuition when selecting colors. The colors you choose reflect your innermost thoughts and emotions.

Metamorphosis

The energies of spring awaken us to life's possibilities. Use the Metamorphosis spread to stir the creative fires within you. Ostara is a playful Goddess. Celebrate fertility, confidence, health, and good fortune as you spread your wings and learn to fly.

If you have a specific question in mind, ask your question as you shuffle the cards. For more information about Metamorphosis, or a specific card in the layout, use one of the three-card

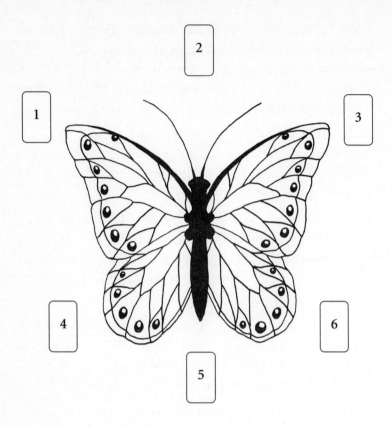

Figure 8: Metamorphosis

spreads found in the second chapter. When you are ready, place your cards in positions one through six, as shown in figure 8.

Position 1: Health. Describes your general state of health at this time. If this card feels negative to you, it is because it depicts an area of healing that needs attention now. The card may also describe actions you can take to enhance feelings of well-being.

Position 2: Good Fortune. Points you in the direction of prosperity. What action can you take to bring the energy of good fortune into your life? A card normally associated with loss, such as the Five of Pentacles, describes a block that may be preventing you from enjoying abundance. For example, the Five of

Pentacles in this position suggests you are overlooking financial resources available to you. No tarot card is "all positive" or "all negative." Every card depicts a spectrum of life experiences, and all cards offer opportunities for change that will release healing energies.

Position 3: Confidence. The self-esteem card. Shows the areas of your life where you are strong. If this card is reversed, it depicts an area of your life that needs attention so your self-esteem can blossom.

Position 4: Career. Describes your thoughts and feelings about work and how your mind is functioning. If a card of energy and movement appears here (such as the Ace, Eight, or Knight of Wands), it describes actions to be taken to improve or strengthen your career.

Position 5: Relationships. Describes your current state of affairs with regard to your emotions and love life. If this card does not appeal to you, it shows where you need to focus your efforts to improve relationships and the emotions associated with them.

Position 6: Metamorphosis. The promise of change. Look at cards one through five. Do you like what you see? Weave together the story of your life in this time of new growth. Where are you strong? By attending to the information in cards one through five, position six hints at the promise of change. It describes the beautiful new you; as you emerge from the cocoon of winter, spread your wings and fly.

To complete the Ostara reading, you can meditate with the cards, write a journal entry, keep the cards on the altar until Beltane, or simply close. Carry a card or two with you during the day to strengthen the connection between you and your heart's desire. Affirm your personal power to stir the creative fires within you: "I am confident and strong. Health and good fortune are mine. This, or something better, is manifesting for me now, for the good of all, harming no one, according to free will. So must it be."

Sample Metamorphosis Reading

Rose feels fortunate to have a sweet daughter and a job she loves, but the winds of change are upon her. She works as a veterinary assistant and adores caring for her four-legged friends. Unfortunately, because of the high cost of veterinary care, the animal hospital is having to cut back on employee benefits, and one cut is health insurance.

Being dropped from a health insurance policy is disastrous for Rose because her daughter is an insulin-dependent juvenile diabetic. She cannot afford the medical equipment and lab tests without insurance coverage; nor can she afford to buy health insurance on her current salary.

Her daughter's father has recently lost his own insurance benefits and is unable to help at this time. He pays child support based on his salary, but it is not enough to buy health insurance. Rose is both angry at the circumstances, and scared of being unable to pay her medical bills.

She decides to do a Metamorphosis reading for insight into her situation. At first, Rose is appalled by her cards. They all look so bleak in this time of renewed energy. Then she remembers that the cards may not tell her what she wants to know, but will always tell her what she needs to know. After meditating, writing in a journal, and looking through her tarot books, she realizes these seemingly "negative" cards are offering her great truths and opportunities to change her predicament.

Position 1: Death. Rose understands that the Death card usually does not predict physical death. It's about transition and permanent change. Death suggests to Rose that she is afraid of the future, and her health is suffering for it. This card asks Rose to release situations and relationships that no longer serve a purpose. It is a call from the inner self to pay attention. The gift of the Death card is metamorphosis. Rose understands that losing or changing her job may be an opportunity in disguise, if she can release the fear associated with it. The Death card reminds her that change is beneficial.

Position 2: Knight of Pentacles. The Knight tells Rose to focus on practical matters. Right now, her good fortune depends on her ability to find money. She's unsure how much money she spends every month. The first thing she needs to do is make a budget and stick to it. The Knight of Pentacles focuses on ways to find and nurture projects that bring in steady income and attract loyal customers.

Rose has always associated the suit of Pentacles with the earth and all her creatures. Because Rose loves animals and has experience working with them, she decides to research how to begin a company specializing in pet-sitting. There is tremendous need in her community for such a service, especially during the warmer vacation months. She knows it pays well, has flexible hours, and requires little start-up expense. She wonders if the Pet Sitters Association might have a health insurance plan.

Position 3: Ace of Swords. The Ace of Swords is a card of strength in spite of adversity. It promises that out of struggle, good will come, and shows that Rose has the power to win by thinking and communicating differently. She has no illusions about her situation, and her realistic outlook is her strength. Rose knows she is strong. She has the ability to make positive decisions based in fact. The Ace of Swords reminds Rose that she can overcome her money obstacles by applying her intellect to problem-solving.

Position 4: Five of Pentacles. This card truthfully describes Rose's thoughts and feelings about her work situation right now. She is struggling with basic survival issues: money, a job without benefits, lack of health insurance, and the emotional hardship of having a daughter with a chronic illness.

The Five of Pentacles also addresses the apprehension and self-doubt Rose feels about starting her own pet-sitting service and being self-employed. She feels that she is alone and she must stand or fall on her own. The Five asks Rose to give herself some time to think her financial situation through. She is tired of worrying about money. The Five of Pentacle promises Rose that if she can hold on, her fortunes will reverse. It also suggests she is overlooking an outside financial resource, like aid for a dependent child.

Position 5: Three of Swords. Rose's intense feelings about lack of health insurance, her work situation, her ex-partner's inability to help, and her daughter's well-being have taken their toll. Rose is deeply distressed.

Like it or not, the Three of Swords tells Rose that change must be made for healing to begin. The Three of Swords suggests that Rose needs to stop wallowing in her misfortune and look inside herself for inspiration. Releasing the old idea that her day job "should" pay health benefits generates the new idea that she can start her own successful pet-sitting business and pay for her own insurance premiums. This card asks Rose to acknowledge her distress, examine it, work through it, let it go, and move on to a better way of doing things.

Position 6: The Emperor. The Emperor goes forth to make his own way and is not dependent upon others for success. The Emperor is logical, with a firm foundation of stability. He draws his energy from fire and governs action. The Emperor tells Rose that her greatest strength is willpower. The more focused her intent to establish her own business, the faster it will become a reality. The Emperor and Knight of Pentacles (in position two) have a lot in common. Rose has organizational abilities and the Emperor suggests she has the "fire power" to create financial success. Through focused intent, Rose has the ability to create a successful, profitable small business. By letting go (Death and the Three of Swords), she has the willpower (Ace of Swords) to find the outside resources she needs (Five of Pentacles) in order to create a practical and highly successful small business (the Knight of Pentacles and the Emperor).

The Wheel turns and the fire burns. You have traveled half your journey in the cycling of time, darkness into light. Chapter 5 completes the Wheel as you explore day into night.

5

Completing the Wheel:
Day Into Night

*I have danced at the Witches' Sabbat on many occasions, and found
carefree enjoyment in it.*

—DOREEN VALIENTE

Beltane: April 30
(May Eve)

Beltane, meaning "Bel's fire," marks the emergence of the young
God into manhood. Bel was a Celtic Sky God or "bright and shin-
ing one." Ancient Celts lit fires in honor of Bel to protect their
cattle from disease and harm. The farmers herded the cattle to
summer pastures until Samhain, when the cattle would once
again return to their pens for winter protection.

Celtic people also celebrated the union of the Stag Lord and the
May Queen. May Poles, symbolizing the God, were adorned with
flowers and greenery, representing the Goddess. Their sexual
union brought fertility to the land for the coming summer
months. Beltane marked a time of vitality, passion, and hope, and
the villagers reveled in dancing, song, feasting, sexual freedom,
and ritual. May Queens are still chosen today in a diluted version
of Beltane. Few mothers and daughters realize the significance of
the role!

Beltane, sometimes called Walpurgis, was the time for couples to dance around the Bel fire in an act of commitment to one another for a year and a day. After that time, they could marry in a ceremony called handfasting, or go their separate ways. Each entered the union knowing they were not trapped. Both knew they could choose not to continue, giving the relationship both freedom and strength.

Modern witches light a fire within a cauldron to celebrate the union of the Great Mother with her young Horned God. Love is in the air. The earth is ablaze with color and life. On Beltane, witches rejoice in the earth's fruitfulness and the intoxicating joy of being alive.

The Beltane Ritual

Fragrant flowers, lush green foliage, and warmer temperatures celebrate the magical energies of love. It is time for splendor in the grass. Beltane is a bawdy holiday of love, sexuality, regeneration, and prosperity. We drink in the earth's colors, aromas, and tastes. Appetites are keen. Beltane energy is powerful, and expectations of the future are high. It is the perfect time to focus on children and safety because spring captures the feeling of being young again.

When worn or placed upon the altar, copper, gold, emerald, malachite, rose quartz, and garnet will enhance the energies of Beltane. After deciding your magical working(s) for Beltane, focus your intention to realize your desire.

Beltane Tarot Cards

Place the Lovers, card 6, on your altar to symbolize commitment and responsible choice in ongoing relationships. The Two of Cups resonates with emotional balance, romance, and passion. The Ten of Cups relates to fulfillment, joy, and contentment in personal relationships. It is a card of emotional safety and security. Use the Page of Cups to represent a child or feeling young again. The King of Pentacles conveys prosperity, and the Empress or Queen of Pentacles celebrates your power to create.

The Scents of Beltane

Any fragrant flower—the choice is yours! Rose incense or oil captures the heady aroma of the season.

Magical Brews of Beltane

Herbs, spring berries, and flowers abound. Try strawberry, elder flower, rosebud, nettle, mint, or catnip tea. Add lemon and a slice of orange, if you like.

Candles of Beltane

Red symbolizes love, sexual passion, awakenings, blossoming, and marriage. Green projects the life force in nature, growth, and prosperity. Use pink or blue for children. Pink also signifies true friendship. White represents security and protection, and sends out the energy of your pure intentions.

May Queen

May is a time of fertility and high spirits. By Beltane, the dark time of the year is a distant memory and the possibilities of life seem sweet. Use the May Queen spread to regain or confirm a sense of abundance and safety. If you have a specific question in mind, ask it as you shuffle the cards. For more information about the May Queen layout, or a specific card in the layout, use one of the three-card spreads in chapter 2. Shuffle the cards and place them in positions one through six, as shown in figure 9.

Position 1: Safety. Emotional security. What you need to feel safe. Where are you secure in yourself? A seemingly negative card describes a situation that needs your focused attention. Work with the energy of that card to produce feelings of safety.

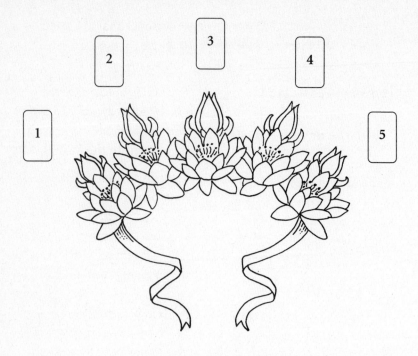

Figure 9: May Queen

Position 2: Abundance. Feelings of plenty. Abundance may encompass monetary prosperity, but it also describes the emotional breadth of your life that is full and sweet. A challenging card directs you to constricted energy flow; by releasing the block of a challenging card, emotional abundance will follow.

Position 3: Regeneration. Exploring the possibilities. The bold action needed to grow and flourish. A challenging card will show you the block that keeps you from your heart's desire.

Position 4: Love. Emotions and relationships. All forms of love, from friendship to sexual passion. Only you know your heart. Look at the suit of the card: What does it tell you about the love in your life right now? (Wands = passion or anger; Cups = love or friendship; Swords = loving the intellect, heartache, or painful decisions; Pentacles = sensuality, the body, or the value you place on love; Court Cards = personal characteristics in your relationships; Major Arcana cards = the big picture, karma, or the spiritual aspects of your relationships.)

Position 5: The Future. The present conceivable outcome based on the flow of cards one through four. What story do the cards tell? The lessons to be learned and the potential for growth. How does position three, regeneration, relate to the future?

Nothing in tarot is preordained, and you always have a choice. If you do not like the cards in this layout, honor the information they are giving you, for they offer great truths. Next, choose other cards that radiate the energy of your heart's desire and place them over the original layout. Focused will remains the core of magic. Refer to chapter 6 for methods of changing the cards to change reality.

To complete the Beltane reading, you can meditate with the cards, write a journal entry, keep the cards on the altar until Midsummer, or simply close. Carry a card or two with you during the day to strengthen the connection between you and your heart's desire. Affirm your power to reclaim abundance and safety: "I focus on the powerful energies of youth. Expectations for the future are high. This, or something better, is manifesting for me now, for the good of all, harming no one, according to free will. So must it be."

Sample May Queen Reading

Erin has a good job as assistant editor of a small newspaper, but her work demands long hours at the office. When she comes home, she is exhausted and just wants to sleep. Her husband Jeff complains that the rigors of Erin's job drain her of energy and she is becoming emotionally distant because of it.

To complicate things, Erin's sister, brother-in-law, and their little girl have temporarily moved into Erin and Jeff's house. They have recently moved from another state and are looking for a place of their own, but things are not moving as fast as expected.

Between the demanding job, her extended family in the home, and a husband who feels neglected, Erin feels overwhelmed. She has plenty of hobbies and interests, but can't remember the last time she had a moment to herself to pursue them. Life is becoming a burden and she has lost the feeling of joy or possibility. Sometimes she wants to run away from it all. Erin decides to do a May Queen spread because she needs to recover a sense of abundance and safety.

Position 1: Nine of Swords. Erin doesn't think the Nine of Swords looks very safe. She realizes it describes a situation that needs her focused attention in order to produce feelings of safety. Erin has problems sleeping because her house is too full, her husband isn't happy, and her job is stressful. While she loves having her family close, the situation bothers her because Jeff is feeling like he's being run out of his own home. She secretly worries that there will be an uncomfortable family scene between her sister and Jeff while Erin is at work. This leaves her with feelings of apprehension.

The Nine of Swords suggests that the problems at home aren't as bad as she imagines them to be. Because Swords are about communication, it's time for Erin to have a talk with her husband to avoid cutting remarks later. The truth of Erin's situation (and direct communication with her family, however painful) will help her recover a sense of safety.

Position 2: Five of Cups. Again, Erin doesn't see the Five of Cups as a card of plenty. The challenge of this card directs her to constricted feelings that block emotional abundance. The Five of Cups is about disappointment, especially in relationships. Erin has a tendency to hold onto painful memories, and the Five of Cups tells her it is time to pick up the pieces and go forward.

The Five of Cups speaks of deep feelings and unhappy memories. Erin must ask herself who is disappointing her most: her husband, for resenting her sister's family; her job, for being so time-consuming; or her sister, for being dependent upon her. It is beneficial to acknowledge deep feelings about each situation and unwise to hold onto unhappy memories. Once Erin examines why she is harboring negative feelings, she will be able to release them and emotional abundance will follow.

Position 3: Four of Pentacles. Erin has never thought of the Four of Pentacles as a card of regeneration. Keeping her home and work life together has been difficult and she feels pulled in all directions. Frankly, Erin is exhausted. In this reading the Four of Pentacles is not about miserliness, but conservation of energy. Erin can't do it all, at home or at work. The card suggests that she conserve her energy and establish personal boundaries if she wants a firm foundation of stability in her life. She must learn how to keep her own counsel, when to speak up, when to say no, and when to back off. The payoff for all this hard work in home and work relationships is regeneration of vitality.

Position 4: The Lovers. The Lovers card is about responsible choices in ongoing relationships. Her relationship with Jeff has been going through a bumpy period, but she doesn't know how to verbalize it. Erin prefers to ignore the situation in hopes it will resolve itself.

Erin feels divided about her predicament. She knows that she works too much and her sister's family living in the same house is interfering with her marriage to Jeff; however, her heart says that as the older sister it is her responsibility to take care of her sister and her family and Jeff should understand that. The Lovers card suggests an honest and gentle conversation with Jeff about the family living situation, but she needs to avoid confrontation. This card compels Erin to make a responsible decision about work or home life, take action, and then move on, secure in the knowledge that her choice is the right one.

Position 5: Ten of Pentacles. The Ten of Pentacles is a card of great contentment, promising a firm foundation of home, family, and career. Erin looks at the story that cards one through four weaves. Every card presents a challenge and an opportunity to grow. If she does the work of facing her apprehension (Nine of Swords), establishing open communication with family members (the Lovers), conserving her energy by establishing personal boundaries (Four of Pentacles), and letting go of resentment (Five of Cups), Erin will experience renewed vitality for life. She is well on her way to reclaiming a sense of safety and abundance.

Midsummer: June 21 (Summer Solstice, Litha)

In the Northern Hemisphere, the summer solstice, or Midsummer, arrives when the powers of nature are at their highest point. This is the longest day of the year; the sun has reached its peak and, in one magical moment, starts to wane. It is the day of Litha, Celtic Goddess of Abundance, Fertility, and Order. While the summer solstice shares many of the carefree qualities of Beltane, Celtic people instinctively knew that the sun's change was an important event.

During the winter solstice, the Holly and Oak Kings wrestle in a timeless battle, and the Oak King wins. At Midsummer, the Holly King, lord of the waning cycle, once again does battle with the Oak King, lord of the waxing cycle. This time, the Holly King triumphs over his rival twin.

Fires of oak wood were lit in honor of the Goddess of Hearth and Home. Committed couples from Beltane leaped the flames to encourage fertility, health, love, and purification. The ashes were scattered in the fields as fertilizer and to ensure good crops.

As with so many pagan celebrations, the element of fire is central to summer solstice festivities. The sun blazes hot and flowers are in full bloom. Today, Midsummer is the classic time for magic of all types, including protection for the home, pets, and all creatures, purifying space against harmful energy, divination, and healing.

Midsummer has long had a reputation of bawdiness and fervor. Celtic people drank ale, made love in apple orchards, and generally behaved in mischievous ways. While the "madness" that Shakespeare wrote of in *A Midsummer Night's Dream* was probably the compound effects of ale, heat, and a full moon, the potent magic of the season lives on.

The Midsummer Ritual

Midsummer celebrates the longest day and shortest night of the year. It shares Beltane's energies of passion and fire—with one big difference: In a single moment the sun starts its descent into winter. On the first day of summer, daylight hours begin to wane until the winter solstice in December. Use the potent energy of Midsummer for magic of all types.

Amber, citrine, cat's-eye, gold, clear quartz crystal, ruby, garnet, and yellow topaz enhance the energies of Midsummer, when worn, carried, or placed upon the altar. After deciding your magical working(s) for the summer solstice, focus your intention to realize your desire.

Midsummer Tarot Cards

Midsummer is a dreamy time of heightened psychic ability. Place the High Priestess, card 2, on your altar for intuition and inspiration. The Queen of Cups excels at metaphysics: clairvoyance, psychic counseling, divination, astrology, and tarot card reading. Use the Queen of Cups to symbolize these abilities in you.

The Tower, card 16, represents the freedom and liberation of summertime. Use the World, card 21, to symbolize the peak experience of fulfillment. Move into a new phase of your life protected by the Six of Swords.

The Scents of Midsummer

All flowers and herbs at the height of their season: Heather, sunflower, rosemary, lavender, iris, magnolia, and honeysuckle are especially attuned to the deep richness of Midsummer.

Magical Brews of Midsummer

The God has reached His maximum power. All drinks that have a "sunny" quality to them, such as orange juice or lemonade, are appropriate. Also, any "warm" herbal infusion, such as mint, chamomile, St. John's wort, vervain, sage, or mugwort tea. Use any brew that speaks to you of summer, hot or iced. (*Note:* St. John's wort has antidepressant qualities and should not be consumed with wine. Mugwort can cause heavy bleeding in some women.)

Candles of Midsummer

Similar to Beltane, except the energy of the sun is the focus. Use red and gold candles to represent fire, passion, freedom, and the heat of summer. Ocean blue, indigo, violet, or purple will link you to psychic ability, and orange attracts that which you desire. Use white for purity of intention and protection.

Midsummer's Dream

Celebrate the freedom and liberation of summer. Because energy is so potent during Midsummer, it is a wonderful time for protection, developing psychic ability, and divination. Use the Midsummer's Dream layout when you want to visualize your heart's desire. Catch a glimpse of the future in the full beauty of the sun's golden rays.

The cards in this layout are read in pairs. (Card one and its future trend, card two; card three and its future trend, card four; card five and its future trend, card six.) If you have a specific question in mind, ask it as you shuffle the cards. For more information about the Midsummer's Dream layout, or a specific card in the layout, use one of the three-card spreads in chapter 2. Shuffle the cards and place them in positions one through six, as shown in figure 10.

Position 1: Freedom and Liberation. What will set your spirit free? What keeps you from your heart's desire? This card indicates

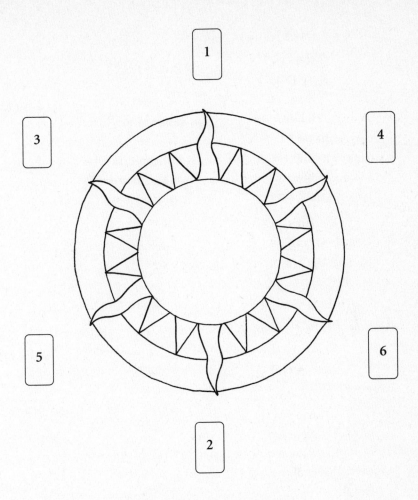

Figure 10: Midsummer's Dream

where energy is blocked or where energy flows the strongest. It shows either your strengths or challenges. Directly facing the challenge allows creative energy to flow toward your heart's desire.

Position 2: Future Trends of Freedom and Liberation. Indicates possible scenarios based on influences at this time. Do you obtain your heart's desire or are you setting up the wrong life?

(*Note:* No tarot reading is a preordained destiny. If you don't like this, or any future trend card in the layout, do a three-card reading for more information and read chapter 6. You *can* change current trends to change the future.)

Position 3: The Need for Protection. Shows your vulnerabilities or where you might block your heart's desire. Can describe any plane of existence: physical (Pentacles); emotional (Cups); psychological (Swords); actions (Wands); personalities (Court Cards); spirituality and karma (Trump Cards). If you like this card, it describes what to keep and nurture.

Position 4: Future Trends of the Need for Protection. Based on influences at this time, what trends are being set? Are you on the path to fulfilling your heart's desire, or do you need to go in another direction? Please see note under position two.

Position 5: Paying Attention to Intuition. Developing psychic abilities. Indicates your receptiveness to the inner voice of wisdom. Intuition always knows what is best for you. Either describes how to develop the inner voice of the soul, or what may be blocking its development. Closely related to position one, setting your spirit free.

Position 6: Future Trends in Psychic Development. Paying attention to intuition is hearing the voice of the soul, and is your most direct path to your heart's desire. Given the influences of the cards at this time, what is a probable outcome to your psychic development? Remember, you can change the cards to change reality.

To complete the Midsummer reading, you can meditate with the cards, write a journal entry, keep the cards on the altar until Lughnasadh, or simply close. Carry a card or two with you during the day to strengthen the connection between you and your heart's desire. Affirm your personal power to develop psychic ability: "I listen to the voice of intuition and clearly visualize my goals. This, or something better, is manifesting for me now, for the good of all, harming no one, according to free will. So must it be."

Midsummer's Dream Sample Reading

Rowan is a massage therapist and amateur astrologer. Despite the energy and optimism of the season, she feels depressed. Her life partner, David, has struggled with various addictions and is now chronically ill because of it. Rowan is supporting both of them.

David is an intelligent man, but he hasn't been able to work for awhile. He has been in and out of hospitals over the last year and doesn't make much of an effort to take care of himself or get well. Because Rowan has attended to his many crises, she has had little time to maintain her business and her client list is dwindling. The bills are piling up. Her life feels chaotic and she is exhausted. She understands that she needs to make some decisions about her relationship and her career.

Rowan knows she can make money as a professional astrologer, but she doesn't have the energy or time to get started. She also realizes she has enabled David to remain dysfunctional because of her great need to rescue and care for people.

Rowan has been giving her power away. She decides to do a Midsummer's Dream layout to take her power back. When she first sees the cards, she is tempted to call the layout a Midsummer's Nightmare, but she remembers that the cards tell the truth. She notes that three of the six cards are from the Major Arcana, and takes it as a sign that the Goddess wants to speak with her. After affirming her desire to have a prosperous career and peaceful life, for the good of all, harming no one, Rowan proceeds with the reading.

Position 1: The Devil. This card is about failure to love the self and being in bondage to a negative thought pattern, relationship, or belief. The Devil indicates the issue is power: controlling or being controlled. Allowing oneself to be victimized is just as devilish as being the aggressor. Rowan realizes that she is being controlled by her partner's circumstances; she is a victim in her own life.

The Devil reflects belief in the outer aspects of her life— lack of money, manipulative partner, no time, always a crisis to control—rather than the inner truth of her situation. David isn't going to change and she can't make him better. She is trapped to the substance abuse just as much as David. The Devil represents fear of change and feelings of powerlessness. The chaos in Rowan's life has been making decisions for her. She feels trapped in an inertia that threatens to drag her down. The opportunity that the Devil presents is that when our fears are faced, great growth occurs. Rowan can choose to do things differently. Her transformation will begin the moment she affirms her intention to cast out negativity and replace it with positive action.

Position 2: Eight of Swords. Rowan sees that if she continues on the path of position one's energy, she will be afraid to break free of the chains that bind her. She will be in a mental prison, full of insecurity. Although she feels she is in an impossible situation, there is a way out. These two cards together indicate that the way is not easy, but the Devil and the Eight of Swords offer tremendous opportunity for growth because they emphasize the power of personal choice. Nothing prevents Rowan from leaving an oppressive situation except her own negative beliefs. If she changes the belief of powerlessness (I can't do anything about the chaos) into a belief of choice (David will find his own truths without my rescue), she can take her power back.

Position 3: The Magician. Rowan immediately recognizes the Magician as her partner, David. The Magician, in his darker aspects, is the trickster, the con man, engaged in deceit. The shadow side of the Magician is one who dominates those who are easily dominated.

This card asks Rowan to presume there's more here than meets the eye. Paired with the Devil in position one, it confirms Rowan's suspicion that David is still using.

The Magician tells her that *now* is the time to take a stand, visualize a better life for herself, and get to work making it real. Focused will is the core of magic.

Position 4: Knight of Swords. The Knight of Swords tells Rowan that it is time to focus on communication and take action. The Knight also asks Rowan to freely express her needs and opinions to David. This card reminds Rowan that if she doesn't take action on position three, the Magician, she will feel restless and unsettled for some time to come.

The Knight of Swords can indicate legal, medical, or professional help. The challenges of this card are living through sudden change and dealing with a mind that can hurt another. Rowan is grateful that she can prepare for change. But the Knight of Swords also predicts opportunity—Rowan can use the energy of the Magician coupled with this card to produce a liberating, progressive period. The Knight asks Rowan to seize control of her life and stop viewing herself as a victim.

Position 5: The Moon. The Moon perfectly describes the confusion, anxiety, and insecurity that haunts Rowan. Someone has let her down. At times, she finds it difficult to distinguish reality from illusion. The Moon carries a strong message when in a layout with the Devil—Rowan's feelings of being alone and victimized have produced a spiritual separation from her own wise counsel. She has cut herself off (indicated by the Devil) from the source of intuitive knowing (represented by the Moon). The still small voice only whispers and she cannot hear it above the din of her chaotic life.

It's true. Rowan doesn't take the time to meditate or study astrology anymore. She's stopped painting, something that used to touch her soul. This is the first tarot reading that she's done in months. Rowan has been so busy rescuing her partner that her massage business is in shambles and her astrology consultation service can't get off the ground. She is exhausted, can't sleep, and doesn't remember her dreams. Rowan's first step in taking back her power is to take the time to pay attention to intuition, because it always knows what is for her highest good.

The Moon urges her to deepen her spiritual life to find the answers she's looking for. If she takes the time, she will experience clairvoyance, lucid dreaming, astral projection, or past-life flashes. The Moon promises Rowan that she is going through a phase. Coupled with the Magician, she can look to her dreams, daydreams, and insights to create a positive future.

Position 6: Two of Pentacles. This card suggests change and fluctuation in financial matters, juggling more than one source of income. By heeding the advice of position five, the Moon, Rowan will learn to go with the flow instead of trying to control her partner. The Two of Pentacles indicates juggling, adaptability, and skillful manipulation to achieve success. The change in her life is good as long as she stays flexible within the change. Versatility is her greatest strength.

Rowan is encouraged because the Two of Pentacles also suggests balance and equilibrium. A major change can usher in a new era where mind, body, emotions, and spirit are connected. She decides to do a three-card layout to summarize the reading.

Sample Three-Card Reading

Card 1: The Fool. This card signifies that which is difficult in the present situation. Rowan has problems with trust in the basic goodness of the universe. Sometimes she is naive or gullible, willing to believe lies when she doesn't want to see the truth.

The Fool tells her to take the leap of faith without knowing its outcome. Rowan has always believed that "the devil she knows is better than the devil she doesn't know."

The Fool, in this case, is urging Rowan to directly confront David about his deceptive behavior. Regardless of outcome, the results will be for Rowan's highest good.

Card 2: Queen of Cups. Rowan knows she is a gifted astrologer, counselor, and psychic. She also knows she hasn't been still long enough lately to hear the inner voice of wisdom. The Queen of

Cups reminds Rowan that her gifts will be enhanced if she takes the time to participate in ritual and meditation. Rowan is encouraged to start her astrology consultation service because the Queen of Cups excels in metaphysics.

Card 3: Wheel of Fortune. Even though times have been tough, the Wheel of Fortune tells Rowan that things are getting better. This card reveals the connection between luck and destiny. She doesn't have to remain stuck in place if she embraces the risk and takes the plunge, especially coupled with card one, the Fool. The Wheel of Fortune tells Rowan that there's more to life than the external world. By communicating with her inner self, she will discover the core strength that creates her destiny. Rowan decides to take back her power; she plans to talk with David and read about how to start an astrological consultation service.

Lughnasadh: August 1 (Lammas)

Lughnasadh [loo'-na-saw] marks the beginning of the grain harvest, the first harvest on the Wheel of the Year. It commemorates the death and rebirth of the Celtic Sun God Lugh, God of Agricultural Fertility. The celebration is also known as Lammas, a medieval Christian name meaning "festival of bread," August Eve, Feast of Bread, and Harvest Home.

As the Sun God loses his strength and begins His southward journey into winter, the days become shorter and the nights grow longer. The importance of grain to life in an agricultural society cannot be overemphasized. Ancient people knew that a poor harvest meant certain death in the harsh winter months. To ensure plentiful crops, great celebrations and thanksgiving offerings were dedicated to Demeter, Goddess of the Earth, and Ceres, Goddess of the Harvest. The English word "cereal" comes from Her name. Farmers attended wakes to honor the death of the Grain God. They knew that, as the God was dying, He would be reborn of the Mother at Yule, as winter transformed itself once again into spring.

Lughnasadh is a time of bounty, and the Goddess wears a face of abundance. We reap the benefits of fresh fruits, vegetables, and herbs. Witches remember summer's warmth, as the sun is in His last mighty display. Although summer is hot and lush, signs of the sun's waning strength lie just around the corner in autumn's golden leaves. The sun is changing and it is beneficial to ground and connect to Mother Earth. Lughnasadh is also a time to practice patience, trusting that the Goddess will provide. During the first harvest, witches are reminded to attune to nature and her cycles.

Lughnasadh Ritual

Lughnasadh, the First Harvest, is a time to remember that nothing in the universe is constant except change itself. As the Lord of the Grain plans to journey to the land of eternal summer, the Goddess teaches the secrets of rebirth. Offer thanks for the continuing cycle of life on earth.

When worn or placed upon the altar, moss agate, aventurine, golden topaz, obsidian, lodestone, cat's-eye, clear quartz, and citrine will enhance the energies of Lughnasadh. After deciding on your magical working(s) for the first harvest, focus your intention to realize your desire.

Lughnasadh Tarot Cards

Place the Wheel of Fortune on your altar to symbolize the cycle of life, death, and rebirth. The Queen of Pentacles and the Empress represent the energies of connecting, sharing, fruition, and first harvest. Celebrate your abundance with the Ten of Pentacles. Strengthen career and financial security with the King of Pentacles and the Emperor.

The Scents of Lughnasadh

The plants of spring wither and drop their seeds and fruit for our use. Use any scent that speaks to you of warmth and bounty. Common First Harvest incense and oils include dried rose petals, peony, comfrey, any berry aroma, apple, and sunflower. All grains, seeds, and flowers are appropriate. Decorate your altar with corn, wheat, ivy, acorns, grapevines, marigold, nasturtiums, clover, or goldenrod. Fill your living space with the delicious fragrance of fresh-baked bread.

Magical Brews of Lughnasadh

The Goddess offers many gifts at this bountiful time of year. Use any berry or berry leaf tea such as strawberry, blackberry, raspberry, and blueberry. Other infusions include comfrey and vervain. Cider, pear nectar, and grape juice are attuned to the magic of the first harvest.

Candles of Lughnasadh

Gold or yellow candles represent the sun. A candle for each color of the rainbow symbolizes earth's bounty in full expression. White indicates your purity of intention. *Note:* I remember the colors of the rainbow by an acronym I learned in third grade: *Roy G. Biv.* Starting from the bottom: *R* (red), *O* (orange), *Y* (yellow), *G* (green), *B* (blue), *I* (indigo), *V* (violet). They're also the colors of the chakras, red (first) and violet (seventh).

Harvest Home

Lughnasadh is a time for enjoying the expiring passions of the season. The bounties of nature give of themselves. The symbolic aspects of life-sustaining grain spill over into every part of life as we mix its energies with ours in our continuing quest for wisdom. Use the Harvest Home layout for grounding, career, health, connectedness, and bringing your heart's desire to fruition.

If you have a specific question in mind, ask it as you shuffle the cards. For more information about the Harvest Home layout, or a specific card in the layout, use one of the three-card spreads in chapter 2. Shuffle the cards and place them in positions one through seven, as shown in figure 11. The cards form a grapevine herbal wreath, symbolic of the never-ending circle of life.

Position 1: Grounding. Indicates what you need to do to keep both feet on the ground. This card shows the practicalities of your day-to-day life. How do you function in the mundane world? If it is a problematic card, it shows you where to concentrate your efforts so you can better function in the real world.

Position 2: Career. Attitudes About Work. Are you following your heart's desire, or just surviving? This card may give clues about your true calling as opposed to what you do to survive.

Position 3: Finances. Attitudes About Money. Money is energy. Is your energy blocked or does it flow freely? Do you "deserve" to have money? A challenging card reveals attitudes about money that may be holding you back from abundance and prosperity. Concentrate on releasing the blocks that restrict the flow of money. Note whether card two (attitudes about work) is in conflict with attitudes about money.

Position 4: Connections and Sharing. Describes feelings of connectedness with others. How do you let your "guard" down to share with others? (The real you.) A problematic card illustrates either areas of isolation, based on mistrust, or areas of weak boundaries, based on the need for approval. Do a three-card spread for more information if needed. See chapter 6 for methods of changing the cards to change reality.

Position 5: Health and Healing. This card reveals how you take care of your body and nurture yourself. It may describe an area that is out of balance and needs your full attention. A Court Card indicates a healer of some type or participation in healing activities; Wands, spiritual retreats and energy work, such as healing touch; Cups, emotional counselor, psychic develop-

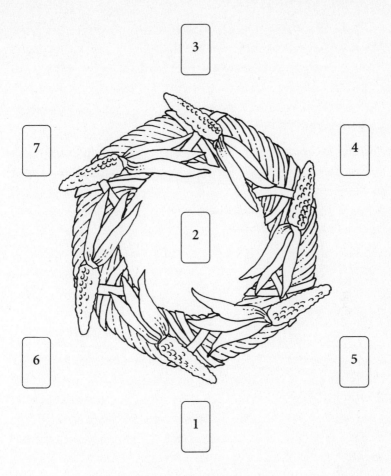

Figure 11: Harvest Home

ment, and dream work; Swords, books or seminars on self-improvement; and Pentacles, nutrition, getting in touch with the natural world, and body work, such as massage.

Position 6: First Harvest. A summing up. You have planned the garden and planted the seeds of your life. What are you reaping for yourself based on your attitudes and behaviors? What are you harvesting? A problematic card indicates an area that needs weeding; it also denotes worn-out ideas or behaviors that are no longer useful to you.

Position 7: Fruition. Achievements, maturation, fulfillment, satisfaction, success. Things that are right with your world. This is the first harvest. What are you thankful for? A challenging card reveals an opportunity for growth that will make you strong. "No pain, no gain," the old saying goes.

To complete the Lughnasadh reading, you can meditate with the cards, write a journal entry, keep the cards on the altar until Mabon, or simply close. Carry a card or two with you during the day to strengthen the connection between you and your heart's desire. Affirm your personal power to bring your heart's desire to fruition: "In my continuing quest for wisdom, I pause and give thanks to the Goddess for Her bounty. This, or something better, is manifesting for me now, for the good of all, harming no one, according to free will. So must it be."

Sample Harvest Home Reading

Olivia is an independent, professional woman. She manages a psychotherapy practice out of her home, specializing in women's issues. Olivia has always thought of herself as the Nine of Pentacles, a financially secure woman, working alone for the good of all. Yet, true to the Nine of Pentacles, she senses something is missing from her life. She has a feeling of restlessness that she can't quite define.

Olivia's psychotherapy practice is not as prosperous as it used to be because of newly imposed insurance constraints. Business has fallen off and Olivia now feels incomplete. She has been a therapist for many years. While she enjoys helping others, she has a secret dream of owning a bed-and-breakfast inn. Olivia sees time slipping away. A nagging sense of isolation compounds the restless desire for dream fulfillment. This surprises Olivia because she has always valued her independence and time alone.

Olivia feels grateful for her abundant life, but senses a need for "something more." She decides to do a Harvest Home layout to examine her attitudes about work, career, money, and connection to others. The first thing she notices about the spread is all of the Pentacles. This tells Olivia that the layout pinpoints what she values. She is surprised, too, about the overall "dreamy" quality of her cards—she has always thought of herself as a practical woman.

Position 1: Seven of Cups. Sometimes called the "fairy dust" card, the Seven of Cups tells Olivia that her feelings of restlessness and yearning come from the inability to make a choice. Usually a woman with both feet on the ground, Olivia's lack of grounding right now is caused by deep indecision. Should she pursue her dream of owning a bed and breakfast, or stay with the tried and true profession of psychotherapy?

Until Olivia chooses one or the other and starts working with it, all her dreams and ideas remain castles in the air. Beneath the confusion lies an abundance of creative energy waiting to be released. Once a choice is made, her sense of grounding will return.

Position 2: Seven of Pentacles. A difficult decision must be made between financial security and uncertain new opportunities. Olivia understands the Seven of Pentacles represents the choice between her established psychotherapy practice (a safe choice) and her dream of operating a bed and breakfast (a choice with the potential to fail). This card symbolizes a practical dreamer— having to choose between material security and a risk that fulfills her heart's desire. It also speaks of sustained effort needed to make her "practical dream" real.

The Seven of Pentacles urges Olivia to make an honest self-appraisal of her options. She realizes she fears failure and needs to assess mistakes to learn from them. The Seven of Pentacles indicates that if she takes herself into deeper levels of awareness, she will find what she truly needs and desires.

Position 3: Four of Pentacles. Olivia has never liked this card. She associates it with miserliness and selfish people. The Four of Pentacles in this position is about fear of depleting resources. Olivia knows that if she sells her psychotherapy practice and invests in a bed and breakfast, she will wipe out her life savings. Even with a loan, the very notion of debt scares her. She has an "ah-ha" moment: As a single woman, money equals security. One of the reasons Olivia has been in such a state of indecision is fear of financial insecurity.

The Four of Pentacles tells Olivia that she is clinging to what is familiar because of fixed ideas of safety and security. These fixed ideas are holding her back from following her heart's desire. Awareness is the key to change, and the Four of Pentacles presents an opportunity for Olivia to loosen up to new ideas, because abundance is infinite.

Position 4: The High Priestess. Olivia associates the High Priestess with intuition, mystery, secrecy, and aloneness. The card confuses her because it is in the sharing position. She looks through her tarot books and calls a friend who also reads the cards. After some journaling, conversation, and reading, Olivia understands the message of the High Priestess: If she remains open to cues from her daily life, her choices will become clear.

Olivia's daily life involves interactions with women. The High Priestess tells Olivia that she will find her answers from a woman's group—if she stays receptive to the cues from daily life. When the High Priestess appears with so many Pentacles, it indicates "practical dreaming," that is, dreaming with a purpose. Coupled with the Seven of Cups (position one), the High Priestess urges Olivia to explore diversity in a group setting, through dreams, meditation, astrology, the tarot, and crystal healing.

The Seven of Pentacles tells her that if she takes herself into deeper levels of awareness, she will find her answers. Because this is "practical dreaming" with a purpose, Olivia decides to do two things that will help her decrease feelings of isolation: (1) attend an enrichment class at the university about changing careers, and (2) organize a support group for women making such a change. She has been alone for too long and it's time to get deeply connected with like-minded women.

Position 5: Queen of Pentacles. Olivia overeats when she worries. The Queen of Pentacles asks her to be aware of nutrition, because we are what we eat. The Queen also reminds Olivia that she is at her best when she nurtures herself and others. This Queen's astrological element is Earth. Olivia will regain a feeling of well-being (and groundedness) if she continues with the activities she loves, despite the period of indecision: cooking, gardening, playing with her cats, getting a massage, taking walks in the park. Olivia will feel most healthy when she allows intuition and logic equal time.

Position 6: Two of Swords. The restlessness that Olivia feels is based on reaching the proverbial fork in the road. She has procrastinated in making a decision between job security and job satisfaction. The impasse or stalemate has caused her great tension. Olivia needs to do some "weeding out": She has a decision to make, and once she makes it, her life will resume its forward momentum.

Because this card is a Two, it speaks to Olivia of balanced thinking and compromise. Nothing is ever black and white. Does she have to completely forsake her psychotherapy practice for a bed and breakfast? Couldn't she combine the two somehow? Even though she will not make the decision right now, Olivia feels better for seeing things in a new light.

The idea of blending contrary things makes Olivia think of the Two of Cups, a loving and healing union of opposites. She places the Two of Cups on top of the Two of Pentacles with great intention and concentration. She knows that changing the cards changes reality.

Position 7: Nine of Pentacles. Olivia smiles when she sees this card. Back to the future, so to speak, for she has always thought of herself as the Nine of Pentacles. She takes great satisfaction in being a strong, independent woman with good self-esteem. She has made her own way and has been rewarded for it. Olivia is reminded that, despite the restlessness and indecision, she has much to be thankful for at this time of First Harvest.

Mabon: September 21
(Fall Equinox)

The autumn equinox is the completion of the harvest begun at Lughnasadh and is considered the witches' Thanksgiving. Day and night are once again equal as the sun passes the equator. From this point on in the Northern Hemisphere, the nights grow longer until the winter solstice in December, when the Sun God is reborn and daylight hours increase once more.

The full moon closest to the equinox is called the harvest moon. It rises for several days around sunset and provides longer moonlit evenings than at any other time of year. Corn was a New World product, unknown to Celts, so in lieu of corn, Celtic people cut down grain during the light of the harvest moon, and harvest suppers were held as the last of the grain was safely stored. They also made grain dolls to pay homage to the spirit of the Grain King. The grain dolls were either made in the image of the Great Mother, or fashioned into symbols of sexual prowess, such as horns and cornucopias.

Mabon is a time of balance, harmony, and change in the sign of Libra. There is briskness in the air. Nature draws back her bounty, getting ready for winter and a period of rest. The fall equinox is a bittersweet stop on the Wheel of the Year. As the Celtic God Mabon prepares to leave his physical body and explore the unseen world, He blesses us with autumn, the most beautiful season of all.

After Mabon, we find ourselves once more at Samhain. The Wheel turns and the never-ending cycle of life, death, and rebirth begins again.

Mabon Ritual

At Mabon, once again, day and night are equal. From this one moment of balance, hours of darkness lengthen until the sun is reborn at Yule. Mabon is a time of balanced and harmonious energy, but with a sense of anticipation and change in the air.

Amber, yellow topaz, peridot, gold, copper, bronze, citrine, and cat's-eye will enhance the energies of Mabon when worn, carried, or placed upon the altar. After deciding on your magical working(s) for Mabon, focus your intention to realize your desire.

Mabon Tarot Cards

The astrological counterpart of Justice is Libra, the scales. Place Justice on your altar as a sign of balance, harmony, and the ability to make adjustments. (Justice is card 8 or 11, depending upon your deck.) Judgement, card 20, is an advanced Libra card. As such, it symbolizes the compassion and order that results from understanding cause and effect. Use Judgement to represent taking stock and reaping the harvest. As the nights grow longer, attract health and prosperity with the Sun (card 19). Mabon is the witches' Thanksgiving; celebrate your bounty with the Three of Cups.

The Scents of Mabon

Autumn is in the air. Use any fragrance of the season that appeals to you. Some of the most common aromas for Mabon incense and oils include rosemary, sage, basil, pumpkin, cinnamon, clove, apple, and frankincense. Decorate your altar with acorns, gourds, dried leaves, wheat stalks, and corn. Fill your living space with the irresistible scent of fresh-baked corn bread.

Magical Brews of Mabon

The magical brews of Mabon are much like the infusions of Samhain, but less pungent. Apple, chamomile, or rose hip teas taste like earth's bounty. Apple juice and mulled cider with spices such as cinnamon and cloves are attuned to autumn. Add a cinnamon stick to your magical brews to enhance the energies of the season.

Candles of Mabon

As nature draws back her bounty, the vivid colors of summer begin to fade, changing into darker shades of brown, copper, golden yellow, and russet. Use gold to symbolize the dying sun, orange to attract vitality and good health, deep green for prosperity, brown for blessing home and animals, dark yellow for intellectual pursuits or returning to school, and white for protection and purity of intent.

Balance of Power

The hours of day and night are equal at Mabon, and spring is impossible without the second harvest. Autumn is both exciting and sad. During Mabon, think of the lost summer sun and the cold days of winter ahead. Are you ready to face change? Fall is in the sign of Libra, and the Mabon tarot layout is the shape of scales. Use it when you want to find your "balance of power."

The Balance of Power spread looks at your inner and outer focus to life. It compares your ego, will, drive, and sense of personal power to your attitudes, thought patterns, emotions, and feelings of powerlessness. The cards are paired as such: 1–2, 3–4, 5–6, and 7–8. To get the most from the Balance of Power reading, look for conflicts within the pairings. Great diversity between the energies of the paired cards represents areas of tension and conflict, producing feelings of imbalance that lead to ill health or disease. See chapter 6 for methods of changing the cards to change reality. By focusing on the cards with the most conflict, you will restore the balance of power.

If you have a specific question in mind, ask it as you shuffle the cards. For more information about the Balance of Power layout, or a specific card in the layout, use one of the three-card spreads in chapter 2. Shuffle the cards and place them in positions one through eight, as shown in figure 12.

Position 1: Taking Stock. Describes your strengths or weaknesses. Think of position one as your "awareness" card and the first step to restoring balance. Tarot tells you what you need to know, not necessarily what you want to know. This card depicts an honest self-appraisal of your life at this time. If you like the card, it indicates what to keep and where you are strong.

Position 2: Giving Thanks. Blessings, however small. As mentioned previously, Mabon is the witches' Thanksgiving. Sometimes in the din of "busyness," we forget that magic lies just beneath the surface of everyday life. Has a butterfly landed on your arm lately? Has a bird serenaded you with a beautiful song? Note whether there is any conflict between card one and two.

Position 3: Personal Balance, Inner Focus. Attitudes, thought patterns, emotions, or feelings of powerlessness that may cause your life to be out of balance. If you like this card, it describes what to keep and nurture. A strength.

Position 4: Personal Balance, Outer Focus. Will, ego, drive, motivation, sense of personal power. A problematic card indicates where you are giving your power away in daily living. Compare the energies of cards three and four. Great diversity between emotion and will denotes stress and tension, and being out of balance.

Position 5: Prosperity, the Inner Focus. Examines your attitudes, beliefs, and feelings about money and abundance. A challenging card indicates where energy is constricted and money or abundance is not able to flow.

Position 6: Work and Career, the Outer Focus. Explores your will, drive, ego, and motivations surrounding work and career. Note whether there is any conflict between cards five and six. Is your attitude about money holding you back? Conversely, are you driven to succeed without your heart being in your work? If cards five and six are in agreement, say both are Pentacles or Cups, then chances are good you have unrestricted energy flow and are following your heart's desire. At least, you are happy where you are.

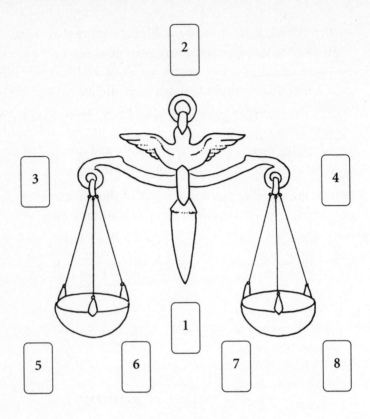

Figure 12: Balance of Power

Position 7: Protection, Inner Focus. Examines attitudes, emotions, or beliefs that lead to feelings of vulnerability and powerlessness. The "stuck place," or area where you may feel victimized. A problematic card reveals a situation that needs your attention now so you can take your power back. Change the cards to change reality.

Position 8: Health, the Outer Focus. Shows the area of your life that is displaying the greatest degree of imbalance. Sometimes it easier to be "sick" than it is to change negative thought patterns and beliefs. For example, getting the flu is an easy way to take time off for rest; it's much harder to ask the boss for a few vacation days or to say no when we are overloaded.

Note whether there is any conflict between cards seven and eight. How do the inner feelings of powerlessness contribute to the outer focus of physical health or illness? Problematic cards show areas of your life that require your attention. Get professional help if you need it. If you like these cards, they reveal what to keep and nurture and where you are strong. Imbalanced energy means being out of balance and can lead to disease. Balanced power equals health and well-being.

To complete the Mabon reading, you can meditate with the cards, write a journal entry, keep the cards on the altar until Samhain, or simply close. Carry a card or two with you during the day to strengthen the connection between you and your heart's desire. Affirm your personal power to face change: "I am calm, strong, and centered. I understand the ebb and flow of life and make adjustments accordingly. This, or something better, is manifesting for me now, for the good of all, harming no one, according to free will. So must it be."

Sample Mabon Reading

From all outward appearances, Haley has it all: a successful career as manager of a computer software company, a beautiful home, many friends, a loving husband, and two well-adjusted teenage daughters. Haley thinks of herself as the Queen of Wands, the "modern woman" of tireless versatility, successfully juggling career, family, and social life.

Haley is a human "doing," rarely taking the time to slow down for introspection and rest. Every hour of every day is filled with work, family, or social commitments. She is a "joiner," and volunteers for all known causes because she has not learned how to say no. To compound her already busy life, she is working part-time toward a mandatory Masters degree in Business Administration to advance within the computer company.

Haley's health is suffering. She has high blood pressure and is on medication. Her heart is irregular. She eats fast food at odd intervals, has no time for exercise, and has gained weight because of it. Haley has no part of a day that she can call her own. On her last birthday a friend gave her a gift certificate for a tarot reading—as a joke. Haley doesn't believe in such nonsense, but she hates to see money wasted so decides to make an appointment for the reading. The bookstore is on her way to class anyway, so why not amuse herself? After listening to Haley for a few minutes, the reader decides to do a Balance of Power layout.

Position 1: Ten of Wands. The workaholic card. The Ten of Wands indicates Haley is not aware of her personal limitations, takes on too much responsibility, and then becomes angry with herself or resentful toward others for doing so. The transformation of the Ten of Wands comes with the realization that limitations are self-imposed. Creative energy will be released when Haley learns to say no to overcommitment, begins to delegate responsibility, and is honest with herself about what she can and cannot do. The Ten of Wands also suggests that Haley has been unable to prioritize what is important and what she can release.

Position 2: Page of Cups. Even Haley, the tarot skeptic, has to smile when she sees this card. The magic of her everyday life is that she has two wonderful daughters. Haley realizes that she takes them for granted; they tend to be mere background noise against her grueling job and graduate school schedule. She promises herself to spend some time with the girls, who are becoming women right before her eyes.

Comparing cards one and two shows Haley that by being on overload, she is missing what is really important, the loves of her life.

Position 3: The Tower. The Tower reveals that Haley is afraid her life will somehow crumble down around her if she changes the way she views the world. To Haley, the Tower represents the frightening chaos of change. Sudden and unexpected change forms the core of the Tower's meaning. But if Haley wants to be honest, she knows that the change will occur because of an inner urge to break free from worn-out belief systems that have kept her imprisoned. If she cannot consciously make changes to restore balance in her life, her unconscious will do it through ill health. The promise of the Tower is that after the breakdown of old, limiting attitudes, new doors will open, ready or not.

Position 4: The Hanged Man. The Hanged Man suggests that Haley is giving her power away because of a refusal to do things differently. This refusal (her "stuck place") has turned her life upside down with exhaustion and ill health. The promise of the Hanged Man is a time of greater understanding without the need to control. By sacrificing her drive to be all things to all people, Haley will no longer be "hung up" by old behaviors that no longer work.

Comparing cards three and four, Haley realizes that she has been hung up by fear of changing the status quo. By looking at things differently (the Hanged Man), she will be liberated from the behaviors that are making her out of balance and unhappy (the Tower).

Position 5: Six of Wands. Haley has long believed that if something is truly successful, there is public acclaim. She admits to the reader that she wants to be admired, even famous. Her sense of abundance comes from the outward approval of others. She likes honors, awards, letters of praise, and public recognition, for they represent a tangible measurement of her worth. In Haley's mind, outer trappings of success equal personal satisfaction and prosperity. She sees drive and ambition as the keys to happiness.

Position 6: Nine of Wands. Haley sees that there is a price to pay for her drive and ambition. The Nine of Wands suggests feelings of being at the end of her rope. The promise of the Nine is that she has strength in reserve. Haley is a strong woman, and the Nine of Wands suggests that her wise use of power should come from learning self-control.

The Nine of Wands is conducive to ill health. It speaks of depleting personal resources. By comparing cards five and six,

Haley realizes that she has created her own fate. Propelled by the need for public recognition, she has dipped into her personal reserve of strength. Yes, the combination of cards is complementary, but the fiery Wands warn of personal consequences for burning the candle at both ends. Cards seven and eight offer advice for this situation.

Position 7: Four of Swords, Reversed. The reversed Four of Swords tells Haley that she needs to take some time off to rest and recuperate. When the reader tells her this, Haley immediately protests and reasons she cannot possibly take a vacation now. The reader responds by saying that none of this will matter if Haley's health deteriorates, and physical health is Haley's most vulnerable area right now.

The Four of Swords in position seven offers advice for restoring balance to Haley's life: take time off to think, rest, and prioritize. Haley needs time for introspection, to lay aside big plans, and heal and renew herself. If she doesn't do it now, she may be forced to do it later, especially when coupled with the Tower in position three.

Position 8: Temperance. The reader tells Haley that Temperance is the healing angel of tarot. The message of Temperance is moderation in all things, easy does it. Temperance is a card of challenging oneself to grow, knowing limits, recognizing resources, and asking for help. Haley has already proven to the world that she is an overachiever. Her greatest challenge (test) to the balance of power is knowing when to say no, delegating responsibility, letting go of the need to control, setting limits, and finding magic in everyday living.

By comparing cards seven and eight, the message is clear: Does success mean having a high-powered job at the risk of losing her health, or can Haley be happy in a lower-profile setting, enjoying time off with her family while in good health? Only she can answer that question, but she leaves the reading feeling empowered and puts in a request for a vacation. Haley has a lot of thinking to do.

You have now completed the journey in the cycling of time, day into night. Chapter 6 explores ways to dedicate yourself to the magical study of tarot.

6

A Year and a Day

That which you are seeking is causing you to seek.

—CHERI HUBER

The addition of leap day, or adding an extra calendar day every four years in February, probably gave rise to the phrase "a year and a day." A year and a day has always been considered a magical span of time, used in all sorts of pagan customs. The traditional period of study for initiation into the Old Religion of the Goddess was a year and a day.

You can keep this ancient custom by studying the profound meaning of the Wheel of the Year and its relationship to the universal symbolism of tarot. For example, begin a ritual of entering Crone's Wisdom on Samhain this year and end with a celebration of completion next year on November 1.

Another idea is to begin a ritual of entering a fertile, creative time of your life on Beltane this year and end with a celebration of completion next year on May 1. During this period, focus on ways to release your creativity through the study of tarot. You design the rituals. Use the ones described in this book as suggestions to get you started.

As you go through the initiatory period of a year and a day of tarot study, learn as much as you can from books and teachers. I have heard it said that when the student is ready, the teacher will appear, but I offer another version of this wise saying: When the teacher is ready, the student will appear. Be sure to make your own impressions the starting point of your studies, and do only those things that feel right to you.

Besides studying tarot, you can use the cards for magical spells. As Rachel Pollack reminds us, "Change the cards, change reality."[1] Tarot cards are your earthly connection to your spirit's desire. Select the corresponding Esbat or Sabbat to begin a period of focused tarot meditation as it relates to your need or desire. Because tarot card images are not static, they form a symbolic picture of your intention.

Tarot can help you to train and exercise your will. Using tarot for magic works two ways: You can either pick a card, or group of cards, to symbolize your desire, such as the Ace and King of Pentacles for making money; or you can work with a card from a layout that makes you uncomfortable. Let's say you have the Three of Swords in a layout, symbolizing your emotional conflict or painful decision. What would happen if you placed the Star, a symbol of your hope for the future, on top of it? Nothing, if you did so without thinking.

But what if you placed the Star on top of the Three of Swords with great intention, as a way of shaping your reality? An idle gesture of playing with tarot cards becomes a deliberate act of will; it becomes an act of magic. Read Janina Renée's wonderful book *Tarot Spells.* It is the best book I have ever read on the use of magic, ethics, and tarot.

When working with spells, be sure to include "for the good of all, harm none, its equivalent or better, according to free will, so must it be." A friend of mine learned this lesson the hard way. Her dilapidated old house was falling down. She needed money to buy a new house and performed a spell for making money, without including the phrase "for the good of all." She got her money—

from the insurance settlement when her old house burned down. She lost everything inside the house that was dear to her, including her beloved cat. Be careful *how* you ask for something because the universe is paying attention.

As you visualize your goal and focus your energy, send yourself down into the card to release its specific energy into the universe. Let go of the outcome—the Goddess may have something in store for you that is grander than anything you could imagine on your own. Be sure to include the following phrase: "This, or *something better*, is manifesting for me now." You can leave the cards on your altar for awhile to strengthen the connection between you and your magical intention.

May the Goddess be your guide as you find the path for learning, using, and loving tarot. Bright blessings to you in all the seasons!

Appendix

Engaging the Magic
of Self-Discovery

If you look at basic tarot texts, you will notice many ways to organize a deck. Some authors put all like numbers together, regardless of suit. In this example, you would find all the Aces, then all the Twos, all the Threes, and so on. Other writers separate the Court Cards so the four Pages, the four Knights, and so forth, are in succession. I have chosen to keep suits together, regardless of numbering. In other words, every Wand appears consecutively, starting with the Ace and ending with the King, as do all the Cups, and so on.

The phrases immediately to the right the Major Arcana card names describe the spectrum of life experiences each card suggests. The first is the card in its highest vibration; the second phrase depicts the card's energy at its most challenging. For instance, the Fool is **Trust/Mistrust.** No card is all "good" or all "bad," and every card represents an opportunity to learn about ourselves. In this example, think of it as a sliding scale of very trusting to not trusting at all. Most of us fall somewhere in the middle of these two opposites, depending on the situation. It's up to us to decide how a card's energy is manifesting itself in our lives at the moment of the present reading.

Not all the meanings of a card will pertain to your situation. Choose one to three phrases that "ring true" and work with them first. As a rule, a tarot card will either tell you about a situation or give you advice about a situation. Consider your *own* insights, meanings, and images, and how they might apply to your life.

I personally do not use traditional reversed card meanings because I interpret a reversed card as being the most important card in the spread, having the "need for" that specific quality or one that is operating at a deeply unconscious level, unknown to the seeker.

Because many readers do assign reversed card meanings, I have included them here for your convenience.

Remember that tarot authors don't agree on the reversed card meanings. Don't take my word for it—I don't have all the answers. Read tarot books, explore, ask questions, work with the cards. Decide what makes sense to you—and trust your intuition in the process! The magic of self-discovery does not come from the cards; the magic comes from you and your willingness to explore your life.

The Major Arcana
(Greater Secrets)

The Fool (0) Trust/Mistrust

Upright: Having an openness to divine guidance based on trust; having spontaneity and a sense of playfulness; willing to take risks and try something new without knowing the outcome because you trust the process; abandoning old ways of thinking.

Reversed: Not listening to your inner voice; fearing or doubting the future; having a blind naiveté (immaturity or foolishness) that allows others to take advantage of you; refusing to try the new; lacking playfulness.

The Magician (1) Focus/Lack of Focus

Upright: Being able to prioritize and make a choice; being able to focus your energy effectively to accomplish your goals; the ability to visualize your goals clearly; discovering the creator within.

Reversed: Lacking focus; indirectness; abusing power for selfish gain; at the worst, the Magician is dishonest about motives and can be destructive in relationships.

The High Priestess (2) Intuition/Superficiality

Upright: Having complete faith in your intuition; making logical decisions based on your intuition; involvement with a group of women; seeking hidden knowledge through dreams, images, feelings, art, tarot, or astrology; seeking a counselor to help you explore things unseen.

Reversed: Being too literal or intellectual; an inability to trust intuition; an inability to acknowledge the masculine/feminine aspect of the personality; being vague or so caught up in your intuitive nature that you have difficulty living in the real, day-to-day world; disliking women.

The Empress (3) Mothering/Smothering

Upright: The archetype of the Great Mother; now is the time to establish yourself in relationship to others; the Empress is the part of you who knows how to create what you need; a time to nourish yourself as well as others; the creator within; a time to get in touch with your body and sensuality.

Reversed: Being a controlling, powerful woman; so focused on others that self-nurturance is neglected; being unable to let go of relationships; emotional neediness; dwelling on the pains of the past; holding on to destructive situations and relationships.

The Emperor (4) Stability/Rigidity

Upright: Building something real and solid; assertiveness; having a clear-eyed view of reality; giving form and structure to your life; accepting responsibility for your actions; using logic to problem-solve; loving father figure; leadership abilities, especially at work.

Reversed: Being disenchanted with life; out of touch with feelings; rigidity; aggression; controlling father-figure; stubbornness.

The Hierophant (5) Inner Conscience/Fanaticism

Upright: Having an inner conscience; searching for a spiritual or personal philosophy that is accessible through word, book, lecture, or service; having a carefully thought out and studied personal philosophy that guides you rather than rules you.

Reversed: Intolerance toward people whose religious viewpoint differs from yours; adopting principles without thinking them through; going against your true beliefs in order to gain acceptance of a group; blind faith; lacking an inner guide.

The Lovers (6) Responsible Choices/Disharmony

Upright: Understanding that both the intellect and intuition are important for guidance; making responsible choices, especially in relationships; becoming aware of the loving nature of your Higher Self; making a responsible decision about a love relationship; looking to your Higher Self for guidance; the ability to negotiate.

Reversed: Being unable to make a choice; feeling cut-off from guidance; not loving yourself; choosing irresponsibly; refusing to look at life's opposites; unable to trust love or risk losing control.

The Chariot (7) Inner Control/Inner Conflict

Upright: Solving a present problem using the skills of your past experiences; resolution of quarrels and conflict; self-control that is based on introspection; seeking to express the soul outwardly through work.

Reversed: Not understanding or controlling the opposites within you; inflated ego; lack of self-control; not having a sense of direction in your life; wanting to control others; aggression.

Strength (8) Compassion/Rage

Upright: Making peace with the dark side of your nature and extending that compassion to others; having courage, strength, and self-discipline; psychic centers are about to open; having an inner strength that allows you to heal yourself and others.

Reversed: Lack of courage or integrity; destructive aggression; rage, possibly expressed in abusiveness or sexual abuse; lack of compassion; denying or being afraid of your instinctual (or animal) nature.

The Hermit (9) Self-awareness/Fear of the Dark

Upright: Seeking solitude to find inner strength; accepting the natural rhythm of life, including aging and death; finding an individual light when established religions fail you; a spiritual climb that makes you a lantern in the dark for others; seeking the advice of a psychic, tarot reader, or astrologer; having inner wisdom; using meditation as a means to understanding; finding a mentor and learning from her experience.

Reversed: Fear of isolation and boredom; fear of introspection; spiritual emptiness; overdependence on a psychic counselor, tarot reader, or astrologer; unable to accept aging or death; impatience; depression; indecision.

Wheel of Fortune (10) Accepting Change/Blame

Upright: Understanding that there is an orderly plan behind the seemingly random changes of your life; accepting the cyclical nature of time and change; a fortunate new beginning; seeing opportunity; determining how past events affect your present situation.

Reversed: Believing yourself to be a victim of fate; feeling stuck in a rut; fighting change; not recognizing opportunities; unable to finish what you start; missing the big picture; holding on to the past.

Justice (11) Balance/Imbalance

Upright: Having the ability to make adjustments in your life; weighing and balancing difficult decisions; setting things right; seeking legal advice; if you've been ignoring what needs to be done, Justice will bring it into consciousness and you'll have an opportunity to take appropriate action.

Reversed: Leaping to a hasty decision without weighing all the factors; lack of balance in your life; using only cold logic to make a decision; not being able to weigh and balance difficult decisions; prejudice; being illogical.

The Hanged Man (12) Humility/Pride

Upright: Being able to look at something from another angle; being willing to make a sacrifice for a larger goal; deliberate turning toward the Higher Self and asking for help; allowing things to happen without the need to control; understanding that a reversal of fortune can challenge you to grow stronger.

Reversed: Being "hung up" by circumstances in which old behaviors are no longer working; rigidly holding on to old values; an unwillingness to make the necessary sacrifices or do the work necessary for success; sacrificing too much of yourself.

Death (13) Transformation/Stagnation

Upright: Letting go of the old to make way for the new; being comforted during a sad time with valid insights; being open to change and the opportunities it brings.

Reversed: Blocking out sad feelings; fearing change and allowing that fear to control you; physical or mental stagnation.

Temperance (14) Easy Does It/Overindulgence

Upright: Striving for emotional balance; knowing your resources; deciding to do something because you want to test yourself; taking a moderate approach—easy does it, but do it; allowing the healing process to unfold in its own time; the healer within.

Reversed: Not allowing emotions to flow, so they get stuck in depression or erupt in violence; denying a dialogue between yourself and your higher consciousness; taking action without thought to the consequences; overindulgence and addictions.

The Devil (15) Connectedness/Fear of Separation

Upright: Removing the blocks of fear and separateness; understanding your own light side/dark side, which leads to compassion for others; finding a spiritual life; accepting your need to lighten up and play; learning to love yourself and others; expressing your sexuality with joy; feeling connected to other people and less to material goods.

Reversed: Being chained to your fears; failure to love yourself; being chained to material goods; having an issue with power—controlling or being controlled; separating from your spiritual self; the inability to play; cutting yourself off from others; being the aggressor; repressed sexuality.

The Tower (16) Liberation/Destruction

Upright: Breaking down unhealthy beliefs to liberate your true self; having a flash of illumination; breaking through old ways of thinking; releasing repressed energy that is exciting and dynamic; finding inner strength and spiritual meaning in tragedy and loss.

Reversed: Having false philosophies or old goals that prevent you from seizing new opportunities; avoidance of change; falling apart or breaking down when things change; releasing repressed energy in an angry or destructive way.

The Star (17) Hope/Despair

Upright: An opportunity for new insight into a situation; gaining a sense of direction; having a renewed sense of hope; inspiration; discovering the inner light; the healing heart.

Reversed: Failing to recognize your talents and abilities; loss of hope; loss of self-esteem; getting lost in wishful thinking; lacking faith; lack of self-confidence.

The Moon (18) Mystery/Confusion

Upright: Realizing solutions may be intuitive rather than logical; being open to information from dreams; trusting feelings and intuition; being open to the mysteries of your life; feeling guided or pulled to some predetermined purpose; recognizing the changes and cycles of your life.

Reversed: A time of doubt and confusion about your feelings; a feeling of madness; an uncomfortable fluctuation between feelings; indecision; mood swings; depression; not trusting intuition or feelings.

The Sun (19) Golden Understanding/Burnout

Upright: Success; optimism, positive energy, and action; to become a child again and see the world with joy; calm self-confidence; a time of clear vision.

Reversed: Burnout; burning your candle at both ends; feeling no joy in life; keeping secrets that eventually burn you; overwhelming people with your energy and personality.

Judgement (20) Rebirth/Paying the Piper

Upright: Making amends; paying debts that need to be paid; an honest and sincere self-appraisal; reaping what you have sewn; an integration of the light side/dark side that lifts you into spiritual understanding; compassion; healing.

Reversed: Having a harsh inner critic; seeking revenge or divine retribution on someone who has hurt you; being critical of others; seeking to punish, as in paying the piper.

The World (21)
Soaring to a Higher Overview/Chasing a Rainbow

Upright: The completion of one cycle and the beginning of another; standing on solid ground inside yourself; integration of the shadow; realizing your goals; seeing life as a process; soaring to the higher overview of your life to find its grand theme.

Reversed: Looking for happiness outside yourself; wishful thinking; chasing impossible rainbows; repressing painful memories; hanging on to the past; unable to see the big picture.

The Minor Arcana
(Lesser Secrets)
Wands
The Creative Spirit in Everyday Actions

Element: Fire

Plane of Existence: Creativity, healing action, passion to change, anger, sexuality, spirituality in everyday actions

Ace of Wands: Beginnings; an Upsurge of Energy

Upright: A desire for growth and self-development; passion; inspiration; a spiritual search; rebirth of the spirit.

Reversed: Not trusting your own insight; not trusting your ability to heal; ignoring creative inspiration; too much undirected, fiery energy.

Two of Wands: Balance or the Need for Balance

Upright: A wake-up call for action; the power of choice; change for the better is in the air; harnessing one's personal power to create.

Reversed: A feeling of restlessness; unexpressed creativity; dissatisfaction with life.

Three of Wands: Growth and Expansion

Upright: Initial completion of a project with the potential for expansion; new ideas forming on the horizon; a willingness to explore something new; creating your own future by visualizing it clearly.

Reversed: Problems greater than expected; inability to grasp the higher overview (big picture); unwilling to try something new.

Four of Wands: Stability or Stagnation

Upright: Much-deserved rest after hard work; rite of passage; all is well—for now; harvest home; a time to pause and celebrate.

Reversed: Inability to appreciate success; lack of creative inspiration; failure to express joy.

Five of Wands: Conflict and Struggle

Upright: A sense of rules and fair play; the sharing of ideas in a creative group effort; the willingness to continue with plans and change course if necessary.

Reversed: Feeling the stress of petty obstacles; inner spiritual struggle; following a leader without thinking about the consequences.

Six of Wands: Harmony

Upright: Leadership born of self-confidence; victory/success based on hard work; public recognition for a job well done.

Reversed: Arrogance; looking for shortcuts to success or fame; faking it; insincerity; suspicion of other people's motives.

Seven of Wands: Inner Work

Upright: Taking responsibility for our actions; enjoying competition because it is stimulating and exciting; acting from a position of strength.

Reversed: Being defensive about actions or beliefs; fighting only for the adrenaline rush of being angry; not standing up for ourselves; fighting change.

Eight of Wands: Regeneration and New Ways Forward

Upright: A high-energy card directed toward a goal; a purposeful, productive period after a struggle; responding quickly when the time is right; realization of and using psychic energy to accomplish a goal.

Reversed: Ignoring an uncomfortable situation, hoping it will go away; procrastination; plunging into a situation before being prepared.

Nine of Wands: Completion

Upright: Strength in reserve; the ability to go on no matter what life gives us; recognizing what must be healed.

Reversed: Exhaustion; tension; being at the end of your rope; immobilized by doubt.

Ten of Wands: Starting Over at a Higher Cycle

Upright: Being aware of personal limitations; carrying out responsibilities; *not* carrying the load for irresponsible people; saying no; setting limits; decreasing burdens to conserve energy.

Reversed: Taking on too much, then being angry at yourself for doing it; overburdened with responsibilities; not being aware of personal limitations; unable to say no.

Wand Court Cards
*The Creative/Spiritual Plane of Personality
and Development in Everyday Actions*

Page of Wands:
Messages from the Creative or Spiritual Plane; Risk-taking

Upright: Active imagination; willing to take a creative risk; being on fire with creative passion; having a strong (and healthy) sex drive; being inspired; a creative child.

Reversed: Acting impulsively; refusing to take risks of any kind; being unpredictable; fiery temper; having a feeling of burnout; an ill-tempered child.

Knight of Wands: Focusing on the Task at Hand

Upright: Easy creativity; focused on creative and inspirational pursuits; focused on spirituality; playful; the spirit of adventure; or a person in your life who has these qualities.

Reversed: Taking life too seriously; depression; boredom; lack of discipline to pursue goals; irresponsible behavior; being scattered; or a person in your life who has these qualities.

Queen of Wands: Nurturance and Empathy

Upright: Loyalty; understanding spirituality and the need to be creative; the modern woman: able to juggle career, family, and social obligations at one time; nurturing others and encouraging spiritual growth; intuitive; or a person in your life who has these qualities.

Reversed: Extravagance; pride; vanity; temper; having little insight into spirituality; lack of confidence; self-righteousness; feeling overwhelmed; or a person in your life who has these qualities.

King of Wands: Outer-directed Mastery

Upright: Making decisions based on intuitive flashes of insight; optimistic with a strong sense of self; able to forgive others; having a strong personal spirituality; or a person in your life who has these qualities.

Reversed: Domineering; hot-tempered; impulsive; con man; having selfish motives; bigoted; histrionic; or a person in your life who has these qualities.

Cups
The Emotions

Element: Water

Plane of Existence: Emotions, feelings, intuition, dreams, imagination. (*Note:* Some authors place intuition and imagination with the suit of Wands. You decide whether or not to do this.)

Ace of Cups: Beginnings; an Upsurge of Energy

Upright: The opening of the heart; the opening of psychic, spiritual channels; self-nurturing; new relationships; new feelings.

Reversed: Unhappiness caused by a failure to realize the emotional gifts of everyday life; reacting violently; not recognizing the higher overview

Two of Cups: Balance or the Need for Balance

Upright: Commitment and cooperation in relationships and partnerships; balanced emotions; acceptance of masculine/feminine qualities in our personality.

Reversed: Possessiveness in a relationship; denial of our masculine/feminine personality; inability to commit to a relationship or partnership; uncooperative in partnerships.

Three of Cups: Growth and Expansion

Upright: Time to celebrate; initial emotional work done with much work to follow, but for now, rejoice.

Reversed: Alcohol and/or drug dependence to alter feelings; overindulgence of any kind.

Four of Cups: Stability or Stagnation

Upright: Reevaluation of relationships that yields clarity; reality sets in after a period of idealism, giving way to more realistic expectations.

Reversed: Depression; boredom; resentment; withdrawal from emotions; confusion and hurt; loss of idealism.

Five of Cups: Conflict and Struggle

Upright: Choosing to focus on what is left after loss; seeing that all is not lost; looking within for emotional stability when situations appear to be hopeless.

Reversed: Disappointment on the verge of despair; focusing on loss rather than what is left; staying stuck in regret; wallowing in sorrow.

Six of Cups: Harmony

Upright: Seeing value in the past; making peace with the past in a realistic way. A lover or friend from the past may reappear.

Reversed: Clinging to old ideas; unwilling to change; unable to remember the past accurately because of emotional pain.

Seven of Cups: Inner Work

Upright: Identifying false assumptions; recognizing golden opportunities and taking the time to consider what to do next; recognizing the complexity of emotions.

Reversed: The "fairy dust" card—being stuck in fantasy and wishful thinking; indecision; refusing to grow up (Peter Pan).

Eight of Cups: Regeneration and New Ways Forward

Upright: A painful, conscious act of letting go that takes you deeper into your spirituality; leaving the past behind; letting go of a situation or relationship after a long period of emotional investment.

Reversed: Abandoning hope; a refusal to leave a situation; emotional withdrawal; filling others' needs to the point of exhaustion.

Nine of Cups: Completion

Upright: Sometimes called the "wish fulfillment" card—letting yourself wish for whatever you want, knowing you deserve it; finding solace in ordinary pleasures; optimism.

Reversed: Superficiality; being in a tangled or emotionally oppressive situation; lust; laziness; aimlessness.

Ten of Cups: Starting Over at a Higher Cycle

Upright: Lasting contentment and peace; a gentle love that extends to others; a sense of permanence and future purpose; can indicate marriage and family; being "at home" with yourself and others.

Reversed: An emotionally charged situation produces feelings of anger; failing to appreciate gifts from the heart; too much idealism in personal relationships.

Cup Court Cards

The Emotional Plane of Personality and Development

Page of Cups:
Messages from the Emotional Plane; Risk-taking

Upright: Listening to the heart; the opening of the inner voice; willingness to take an emotional risk because of love; being open to the development and maturation of feelings; or a person in your life who has these qualities; a tenderhearted child.

Reversed: Unwillingness to be open to emotional change; emotionally immature; restlessness; running away from any uncomfortable emotions; fantasizing; or a person in your life who has these qualities; an emotional child.

Knight of Cups: Focusing on the Task at Hand

Upright: Striving for emotional balance; focusing on emotions; the ability to make friends; falling in love; focusing on dream work and having healing dreams; defending your ideals; or a person in your life who has these qualities.

Reversed: Self-absorption; withdrawal from reality to focus on fantasy and daydreams; acting out of emotions; emotional manipulation of others; playboy or playgirl; superficial; or a person in your life who has these qualities.

Queen of Cups: Nurturance and Empathy

Upright: Emotional understanding that nurtures others; sensitivity to emotional pain; loyalty in friendships and love relationships; having psychic skills and understanding they are gifts; emotional maturity; or a person in your life who has these qualities.

Reversed: So immersed in the inner world, the outer world of everyday life may be baffling; emotional possessiveness and jealousy; unfaithfulness in love relationships; unable to tolerate the emotional pain of others; denying psychic ability; or a person in your life who has these qualities.

King of Cups: Outer-directed Mastery

Upright: Feelings under control with a detached awareness; being effective in emotional crises; the wounded healer (healing self by healing others); seeing the humor in emotionally charged situations; or a person in your life who has these qualities.

Reversed: Emotional mistrust; jealousy to the point of rage; hedonism; emotional dishonesty; self-importance; intolerance; emotional weakness; or a person in your life who has these qualities.

Swords

The Power of the Mind

Element: Air

Plane of Existence: Psychological makeup, decisions, depression, conflict, pain, legal issues, loss, communication

Ace of Swords: Beginnings; an Upsurge of Energy

Upright: Victory over struggle; strength despite adversity; the gift of inner vision; an upsurge of mental activity with the power and force to win; change for the good; a card of great spiritual strength.

Reversed: Confused ideas; illusion; emotions controlling decisions; failure to think things through.

Two of Swords: Balance or the Need for Balance

Upright: Seeing the reality of a situation; making a painful decision that allows for change; getting "off the fence" of indecision and taking action.

Reversed: An impasse or stalemate; inability to make a decision; procrastination; not wanting to confront the reality of a situation; blocking emotion.

Three of Swords: Growth and Expansion

Upright: Letting go of something sad or painful; focusing on solutions instead of problems; acknowledging hurt, pain, or grief so it can be faced and worked through.

Reversed: Quarrels and conflict, especially in relationships; a broken heart; blocking the healing process; holding on to old pain; unresolved grief.

Four of Swords: Stability or Stagnation

Upright: Introspection; taking the time needed to heal and renew self; rest and recuperation after stress, especially after surgery; calm after the storm.

Reversed: Denying emotions; hiding from the world to avoid pain or confrontation; not acknowledging the need to rest.

Five of Swords: Conflict and Struggle

Upright: The freedom found in accepting one's own limitations; making an apology; turning away from a struggle; letting go of pride so forward progress can be made.

Reversed: Despair felt after loss; using others as a scapegoat (reason) for our own defeat; not accepting a no-win situation.

Six of Swords: Harmony

Upright: A journey toward peace after an agonizing decision; feeling guided in your decision-making process; making forward progress, especially in the area of communication.

Reversed: Unhappy memories; symbolic of a stormy spiritual/psychological journey; feeling stranded or stuck in deep water.

Seven of Swords: Inner Work

Upright: Using "brains not brawn" in a confrontational situation; prudence; nothing is accomplished by aggression.

Reversed: Using deception to get what you want; dishonesty in communications; avoiding face-to-face confrontation; an unwillingness to ask for help; an impulsive act when careful planning is required.

Eight of Swords:
Regeneration and New Ways Forward

Upright: Letting go of ideas and negative thought patterns that bind; liberation from an oppressive situation due to the courage to see things clearly and take appropriate action.

Reversed: Fear of moving out of an oppressive situation; blocked by your own thoughts; feeling trapped by equally frightening choices; waiting to be rescued.

Nine of Swords: Completion

Upright: Liberation found in confronting your own fears and pain; don't rush things; a little fear is a good thing: Reasonable (healthy) fear helps us survive dangerous situations.

Reversed: The "Nightmare Card"—unchecked fear and negative thought; fear of impending doom; paralyzed by guilt over the past, often with an unknown source; worry.

Ten of Swords: Starting Over at a Higher Cycle

Upright: A final, absolute letting go that allows for growth; coming to terms with what really is, not what one wanted or wished for.

Reversed: Hysteria; hopelessness; being a victim (poor me); an inability to face pain; unable to let go.

Sword Court Cards

*The Psychological Plane of Personality
and Development*

Page of Swords:
Messages from the Psychological Plane; Risk-taking

Upright: Facing fears and depression head-on; being open to intellectual development, study, and learning; developing a deeper understanding of self and personal philosophies. A mindful or quick-witted child.

Reversed: Inaction due to fear or depression; a whirlwind of thought that goes nowhere; making decisions without regard to logic or reason; unwilling to make a decision that involves risk. A depressed or confused child, especially one with attention deficit disorder (ADD).

Knight of Swords: Focusing on the Task at Hand

Upright: Focusing on thoughts, beliefs, and philosophies; focusing on a decision that needs to be made; being versatile and adaptable to change; or a person in your life who has these qualities.

Reversed: Starting projects with excitement and ending them abruptly with chaos; being too impatient to wait for anything; cold logic without feeling; or a person in your life who has these qualities.

Queen of Swords: Nurturance and Empathy

Upright: The one who lives, loves, and loses—and lives to love again. Commonly refers to a widow; spiritual depth caused by prolonged struggle; tolerant and easygoing; political consciousness; or a person in your life who has these qualities.

Reversed: Cold and aloof; unforgiving; rigidity of viewpoint; ultra-critical; failing to balance emotions and rational thought; or a person in your life who has these qualities.

King of Swords: Outer-directed Mastery

Upright: Authority earned through disciplined mental effort; good judgment; lover of truth and justice; fairness above all; diplomatic; or a person in your life who has these qualities.

Reversed: Ruthless quest for power; selfishness; using the intellect to dominate others; pride; arrogance; corrupted authority; or a person in your life who has these qualities.

Pentacles

The Material World

Element: Earth

Plane of Existence: Physical body, instincts, work, money, security, sensuality, home, career, anything of value.

Ace of Pentacles: Beginnings; an Upsurge of Energy

Upright: Being centered; a time to manifest in the material world; financial assistance; a business or work opportunity; the beginning of a new enterprise.

Reversed: Being off-center; having a false sense of security; competitive where money is concerned; feeling stuck; overdependence on security and comfort.

Two of Pentacles: Balance or the Need for Balance

Upright: Adaptability; flexibility; balance; skillful manipulation of many factors to achieve success.

Reversed: Walking a tightrope; feeling out of balance; juggling time; clinging to one position; fake lightheartedness; failing to consider another viewpoint.

Three of Pentacles: Growth and Expansion

Upright: Initial completion of a project with much hard effort to follow; beginning to recognize the spiritual aspects of work; producing something worthwhile; a situation (including health) gradually improving with time.

Reversed: Laziness; not following through on a work situation; a situation (including a health condition) gradually getting worse through neglect.

Four of Pentacles: Stability or Stagnation

Upright: The ability to establish personal boundaries; protection of self; giving life structure; saving money and resources; making every effort count.

Reversed: Miserliness in money or spirit; using money to insulate from the outside world; greed; blocking out feelings; lack of emotional generosity (Mr. Scrooge).

Five of Pentacles: Conflict and Struggle

Upright: Paying attention to detail; something of value is found in a painful situation; through hardship inner meaning is found; realizing help is available and asking for it; climbing back up after hitting bottom.

Reversed: Feelings of abandonment; living with basic survival issues of food, clothing, shelter, and poor health; homelessness; loss of any kind; struggling against problems alone when outside forces are of no help; hitting bottom.

Six of Pentacles: Harmony

Upright: Drawing to you what you need; a healing by giving; sharing and generosity that restores faith; that which we give away returns to us threefold.

Reversed: Feelings of depletion; poor money management; holding someone financially hostage: expecting favors for lending money; insensitivity to the needs of others.

Seven of Pentacles: Inner Work

Upright: Deciding between material security and fulfillment of desire; trusting the process of growth; assessing mistakes to learn from them; being a practical dreamer.

Reversed: Indecision; feeling discouraged; failing to evaluate progress at regular intervals; being in conflict about ambition and other values.

Eight of Pentacles: Regeneration and New Ways Forward

Upright: Apprenticeship; starting over in a new profession; undertaking new work that is meaningful; concentrated effort; changing directions in midlife to find fulfillment.

Reversed: Leaving a job because the work is not fulfilling; being a workaholic with subsequent burnout; ambition without the desire to work hard.

Nine of Pentacles: Completion

Upright: Self-esteem; financial stability that allows for the freedom of meaningful work; a woman who works alone by choice for the good of all; the ability to rely on oneself; finding spirituality in nature and animals.

Reversed: Financially secure, but being without purpose in life; depression; low self-esteem; boredom; imbalance between what we want and what we are willing to work for.

Ten of Pentacles: Starting Over at a Higher Cycle

Upright: Being personally successful while contributing to society as a whole; what you value has lasting value to others; financial stability that builds a solid future; being rich in family tradition.

Reversed: One problem after another; being upset by someone close; lethargy; feelings of separation; the urge to risk everything due to impatience with the status quo; addictive gambling.

Pentacle Court Cards

The Material Plane of Personality
and Development

Page of Pentacles: Messages from the Body; Risk-taking

Upright: Beginning awareness of the need to be slow and patient; being open to learning and preparation; building realistic goals slowly, from the ground up; trusting instincts; listening to what your body is trying to tell you; gaining experience; a patient or practical child.

Reversed: Living a life of excess without having a sense of what is truly valuable; low self-esteem; unwillingness to prepare; holding on to unrealistic goals; being illogical and impatient, ignoring or not trusting instincts; a child prone to excesses in behavior.

Knight of Pentacles: Focusing on the Task at Hand

Upright: Determination; practicality; being completely reliable; perseverance; being able to focus on the important issues; focusing on the body, work, money, or anything that is considered valuable; or a person in your life who has these qualities.

Reversed: Being overly cautious or dogged; laziness; lack of discipline; inability to make plans and carry them out; irresponsibility; lack of imagination; impractical; or a person in your life who has these qualities.

Queen of Pentacles: Nurturance and Empathy

Upright: Love of body; generous and nurturing; in tune with nature and the cycles of life; flexible; allowing others to find their own way; having a healthy relationship with food; or a person in your life who has these qualities.

Reversed: Stubbornness; the need to control; being overly concerned with work or money; finding no value or satisfaction in work; not being able to help or nurture others; hating the body; having an unhealthy relationship with food; or a person in your life who has these qualities.

King of Pentacles: Outer-directed Mastery

Upright: Finding a balance between work and play; being solid, steady, and practical; disciplined; having ambition based on an inner sense of values; being content with what you have; success through hard work; or a person in your life who has these qualities.

Reversed: Being status-conscious and materialistic; distrusting spirituality; greed; slow to change; having a mean streak; being completely out of touch with the body or overly concerned with it—vanity; workaholic; or a person in your life who has these qualities.

Notes

Chapter One: Merry Meet

1. Berube, Margery S., editor. *The American Heritage Dictionary,* Second College Edition (Boston: Houghton Mifflin Company, 1985), 1082.

2. *The New American Desk Encyclopedia,* Fourth Edition (New York: Signet Penguin Group, 1997), 412.

3. Dubois, Marguerite-Marie, editor. *Larousse's French-English/English-French Dictionary,* Second Edition (New York: Simon and Schuster, Inc., Pocket Books, 1971), 390.

Chapter Two: As Above, So Below

1. Gawain, Shatki. *Creative Visualization* (New York: Bantam Books, 1978), 21.

Chapter Three: Enchanted Nights: The Esbats

1. Conway, D. J. *Maiden, Mother, Crone: The Myth and Reality of the Triple Goddess* (St. Paul, Minn.: Llewellyn Publications, 1994), 50.

Chapter Four: The Cycling of Time: Darkness Into Light

1. Cabot, Laurie. *Celebrate the Earth: A Year of Holidays in the Pagan Tradition* (New York: Dell Publishing, 1994), 12.

2. Bowes, Susan. *Life Magic: The Power of Positive Witchcraft* (New York: Simon and Schuster, 1999), 52.

Chapter Six: A Year and a Day

1. Pollack, Rachel. *The Complete Illustrated Guide to Tarot* (Boston: Element Books, Inc., 1999), 182.

Bibliography

Adler, Margot. *Drawing Down the Moon.* Boston: Beacon Press, 1986.

Amaral, Geraldine and Nancy Brady Cunningham. *Tarot Celebrations: Honoring the Inner Voice.* York Beach, Maine: Samuel Weiser, Inc., 1997.

Baldwin, Christina. *Calling the Circle: The First and Future Culture.* New York: Bantam Books, 1998.

Barth, Edna. *Witches, Pumpkins and Grinning Ghosts: The Story of the Halloween Symbols.* New York: Clarion Books, 1972.

Berube, Margery S., editor. *The American Heritage Dictionary,* Second College Edition. Boston: Houghton Mifflin Company, 1985.

Bowes, Susan. *Life Magic: The Power of Positive Witchcraft.* New York: Simon and Schuster, 1999.

Browne, Sylvia. *The Other Side and Back: A Psychic's Guide to Our World and Beyond.* New York: Penguin Putnam Signet Books, 1999.

Cabot, Laurie. *Celebrate the Earth: A Year of Holidays in the Pagan Tradition.* New York: Dell Publishing, 1994.

Conway, D. J. *Maiden, Mother, Crone: The Myth and Reality of the Triple Goddess.* St. Paul, Minn.: Llewellyn Publications, 1994.

Cunningham, Scott. *Wicca: A Guide for the Solitary Practitioner.* St. Paul, Minn.: Llewellyn Publications, 1989.

Gawain, Shatki. *Creative Visualization.* New York: Bantam Books, 1978.

Greer, Mary K. *Tarot for Your Self: A Workbook for Personal Transformation.* North Hollywood, California: Newcastle Publishing Company, Inc., 1984.

Jette, Christine. *Tarot Shadow Work: Using the Dark Symbols to Heal.* St. Paul, Minn.: Llewellyn Publications, 2000.

———. *Tarot for the Healing Heart: Using Inner Wisdom to Heal Body and Mind.* St Paul, Minn.: Llewellyn Publications, 2001.

Johnson, Cait. *Tarot for Every Day.* Wappingers Falls, N.Y.: The Shawangunk Press, 1994.

Larousses's French-English/English-French Dictionary, Second Edition. New York: Signet Penguin Group, 1971.

The New American Desk Encyclopedia, Fourth Edition. New York: Signet Penguin Group, 1997.

Noble, Vicki. *Making Ritual with Motherpeace Cards.* New York: Three Rivers Press, 1998.

Pollack, Rachel. *The Complete Illustrated Guide to Tarot.* Boston: Element Books, Inc., 1999.

Renée, Janina. *Tarot Spells.* St. Paul, Minn.: Llewellyn Publications, 1995.

Starhawk (Miriam Simos). *The Spiral Dance: A Rebirth of the Ancient Religion of the Great Goddess.* San Francisco: HarperCollins Publishers, Inc., 1989.

Index

REACH FOR THE MOON

Llewellyn publishes hundreds of books on your favorite subjects!
To get these exciting books, including the ones on the following pages,
check your local bookstore or order them directly from Llewellyn.

Order by Phone
- Call toll-free within the U.S. and Canada, 1-800-THE MOON
- In Minnesota, call (651) 291-1970
- We accept VISA, MasterCard, and American Express

Order by Mail
- Send the full price of your order (MN residents add 7% sales tax)
  in U.S. funds, plus postage & handling to:
  Llewellyn Worldwide
  P.O. Box 64383, Dept. 0-7387-0105-X
  St. Paul, MN 55164–0383, U.S.A.

Postage & Handling
- Standard (U.S., Mexico, & Canada)
  If your order is:
  $20.00 or under, add $5.00
  $20.01–$100.00, add $6.00
  Over $100, shipping is free

(Continental U.S. orders ship UPS. AK, HI, PR, & P.O. Boxes ship USPS 1st class.
Mex. & Can. ship PMB.)
- Second Day Air (Continental U.S. only): $10.00 for one book + $1.00
  per each additional book
- Express (AK, HI, & PR only) [Not available for P.O. Box delivery. For
  street address delivery only.]: $15.00 for one book + $1.00 per each
  additional book
- International Surface Mail: Add $1.00 per item
- International Airmail: Books—Add the retail price of each item;
- Non-book items—Add $5.00 per item

Please allow 4–6 weeks for delivery on all orders.
Postage and handling rates subject to change.

Discounts
We offer a 20% discount to group leaders or agents. You must order a minimum of 5 copies
of the same book to get our special quantity price.

FREE CATALOG

Get a free copy of our color catalog, New Worlds
of Mind and Spirit. Subscribe for just $10.00 in
the United States and Canada ($30.00 overseas,
airmail). Many bookstores carry New Worlds—
ask for it!

Visit our website at www.llewellyn.com for more information.

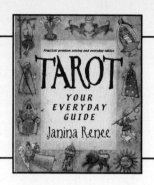

Tarot: Your Everyday Guide
*Practical Problem Solving
and Everyday Advice*
Janina Renee

Whenever people begin to read the tarot, they inevitably find them-selves asking the cards, "What should I do about such-and-such situa-tion?" Yet there is little information available on how to get those answers from the cards.

Reading the tarot for advice requires a different approach than reading for prediction, so the card descriptions in *Tarot: Your Everyday Guide* are adapted accordingly. You interpret a card in terms of things that you can do, and the central figure in the card, which usually rep-resents the querent, models what ought to be done.

This book is especially concerned with practical matters, applying the tarot's advice to common problems and situations that many peo-ple are concerned about, such as whether to say "yes" or "no" to an offer, whether or not to become involved in some cause or conflict, choosing between job and educational options, starting or ending relationships, and dealing with difficult people.

1-56718-565-7, 312 pp., 7½ x 9⅛ $12.95